# 교과부 지정
# 새로 만든
# 영단어 800

기획 : 와이앤엠 어학연구소

그림 : 정수영

## 와이 앤 엠

# 차 례

| a<br>하나의, 한사람의<br>[ə 어] | a a a a a a a a a a a |
| about<br>약, 거의<br>[əbáut어바웃] | about about about  |
| across<br>~의 건너편<br>[əkrɔ́:s어크뤄스] | across across across |
| act<br>행동하다<br>[ækt액트] | act act act act act act |

| [ə 어] | There is a book on the desk. | 책상위에 책이 한 권 있다. |
| [əbáut 어바웃] | What is the book about? | 이 책은 무엇에 관한 내용이야? |
| [əkrɔ́:s어크뤄-스] | My house is across from the park. | 우리집은 공원 건너편에 있어요. |
| [ækt 액트] | He acts like a father. | 그는 아빠인 것처럼 행동한다. |

## address
주소

[ǽdres어드뢰스]

address  address  address

## afraid
무서워하여

[əfréid 어프뢰이드]

afraid  afraid  afraid

## after
~후에

[ǽftər애프터ㄹ]

after  after  after

## again
다시, 또

[əgén 어게인]

again  again  again

## age
나이

[eidʒ 에이쥐]

age  age  age  age

| | | |
|---|---|---|
| [ǽdres어드뢰스] | What is your address? | 주소가 어디에요? |
| [əfréid 어프뢰이드] | I'm much afraid of snakes. | 나는 뱀이 아주 무서워요. |
| [ǽftər애프터ㄹ] | Please repeat after me. | 제 말을 따라하세요. |
| [əgén 어게인] | Do it again. | 다시 해 보렴 |
| [eidʒ 에이쥐] | At the age of 10, I went to Italy. | 열 살 때 저는 이탈리아로 갔어요. |

## ago
~전에

[əgóu어고우]

ago   ago   ago   ago

## air
공기

[ɛər에어ㄹ]

air air air air air air air

## airplane
비행기

[ɛərplén에어플레인]

airplane airplane airplane

## airport
공항

[ɛərpɔ̀ːrt에어포트]

airport   airport

## album
앨범, 사진첩

[ǽlbəm 앨범]

album   album   album

| | | |
|---|---|---|
| [əgóu 어고우] | I met him three years ago. | 3년 전에 그를 만났다. |
| [ɛər 에어ㄹ] | We would die without air. | 우리는 공기가 없으면 죽고 말 거야. |
| [ɛərplén 에얼플레인] | I go to Busan by airplane. | 나는 부산에 비행기로 간다. |
| [[ɛərpɔ̀ːrt에어포트] | Is there a bus of the airport? | 공항으로 가는 버스가 있어요? |
| [ǽlbəm 앨범] | Let's buy him a photo album. | 그에게 사진첩(앨범)을 사주자. |

## all
모두, 전부

[ɔːl 오올]

all   all   all   all   all

## along
~따라서

[əlɔ́ːŋ 얼러엉]

along   along   along

## also
역시, 또한

[ɔ́ːlsou 오-올쏘우]

also   also   also   also

## always
항상, 언제나

[ɔ́ːlweiz 어-얼웨이즈]

always   always   always

## am
~이다

[æm 엠]

am   am   am   am   am

---

| | | |
|---|---|---|
| [ɔːl 오올] | He ate all of the apples. | 그는 그 사과를 전부 다 먹었다. |
| [əlɔ́ːŋ 얼러엉] | Amy walked along the street. | Amy는 길을 따라 걸었다. |
| [ɔ́ːlsou 오-올쏘우] | Tom is kind, also handsome. | Tom은 착하고, 또한 잘 생겼다. |
| [ɔ́ːlweiz 어-얼웨즈] | Mike is always late. | Mike는 항상 늦는다. |
| [æm 엠] | I am a student. | 나는 학생이다. |

6

**ambulance**
구급차
[ǽmbːulɔns
앰뷸런스]

ambulance　　ambulance

**among**
~의 사이에
[əmʌ́ŋ 어멍]

among　among　among

**an**
하나의
[æn 언]

an　an　an　an　an　an

**and**
그리고, ~와
[ænd 앤드]

and　and　and　and

**angry**
화난
[ǽŋgri 앵그뤼]

angry　angry

| | | |
|---|---|---|
| [ǽmbːulɔns 앰뷸런스] | The ambulance is arriving. | 구급차가 도착하고 있다. |
| [əmʌ́ŋ 어멍] | The car is among the trees. | 차가 나무들 사이에 있다. |
| [æn 언] | There is an album on the desk. | 책상에 앨범이 한 권 있다. |
| [ænd 앤드] | I like hamburger and pizza. | 나는 햄버거와 피자를 좋아해. |
| [ǽŋgri 앵그뤼] | Tom looks angry. | Tom이 화난 것 같아. |

## animal
동물, 짐승

[ǽnəməl 애니멀]

animal   animal   animal

## answer
답, 대답하다

[ǽnsər 앤써르]

answer   answer

## ant
개미

[ænt 앤트]

ant  ant  ant  ant  ant

## any
무엇이든

[éni 애니]

any  any  any  any  any

## anyone
누구든지

[éniwʌ́n 애니원]

anyone  anyone  anyone

---

[ǽnəməl 애니멀]   A bear is a big animal.     곰은 몸집이 큰 동물이에요.

[ǽnsər앤써르]   "I'm 8 years old" answered Mike.     "나는 여덟 살이에요"라고 Mike가 대답 했어요.

[ænt 앤트]   The ants are diligent.     개미들은 부지런하다.

[éni 애니]   Do you have any questions?     무슨 질문이 있나요?

[éniwʌ́n애니원]   Anyone can do this.     이런 일은 누구든지 할 수 있다.

**anything**
무엇이든
[énɪθɪŋ 애니씽]

anything   anything

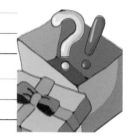

**apartment**
아파트
[əpáːrtmənt
아파-알트먼트]

apartment   apartment

**appear**
나타나다
[əpíər 어피얼]

appear   appear   appear

**apple**
사과
[ǽpəl 애쁠]

apple   apple   apple   apple

**April**
4월
[éiprəl
에이쁘럴]

April   April   April   April

| | | |
|---|---|---|
| [énɪθɪŋ 애니씽] | I can do anything | 난 무엇이든 할 수 있다. |
| [əpáːrtmənt 아파-알트먼트] | I really like my apartment | 나는 우리 아파트가 정말 좋아요. |
| [əpíər 어피얼] | He appears in the room. | 그가 방에 나타났다(들어왔다). |
| [ǽpəl 애쁠] | Do you like apples? | 사과 좋아하세요? |
| [éiprəl에이쁘럴] | I was born in April. | 나는 4월에 태어났어요. |

**are**
~이다
[aːr 아-르]

are　are　are　are　are

**arm**
팔
[aːrm아-ㄹ암]

arm　arm　arm　arm　arm

**around**
~의 주위에
[əráund어롸운드]

around　around　around

**arrive**
도착하다
[əráiv어롸이브]

arrive　arrive

**art**
미술, 예술
[aːrt 알트]

art　art　art　art　art　art

[aːr 아-르]
[aːrm아-ㄹ암]
[əráund어롸운드]
[əráiv어롸이브]
[aːrt 알트]

We are  good friends.
Tom's arm  is long.
I looked around  the village.
Dad will arrive soon.
My favorite subject is art.

우리들은 사이좋은 친구에요,
Tom은 팔이 길어요,
저는 마을 주위를 둘러보았어요,
아빠 곧 도착하실꺼야,
내가 가장 좋아하는 과목은 미술이다,

10

**as**
~만큼
[æz에즈]

as as as as as

**ask**
묻다, 질문하다
[æsk 애스크]

ask ask ask ask ask

**at**
~에서
[æt 앳]

at at at at at at

**ate**
먹었다
[eit에이트]

ate ate ate ate ate

| [æz에즈] | Tom is as tall as I am. | Tom은 나와 키가 같다(톰은 나와 같은 정도의 키다). |
| [æsk 애스크] | Mom asked, "What are you doing?" | "뭐하고 있니?" 엄마가 물어보셨어요. |
| [æt 앳] | I study at home. | 나는 집에서 공부한다. |
| [eit에이트] | I ate bread. | 나는 빵을 먹었어요. |

## aunt
아주머니, 이모

[ænt 앤트]

aunt  aunt  aunt  aunt

## autumn
가을

[ɔ́:təm 어–틈]

autumn  autumn

## away
떨어져서, 멀리

[əwéi 어웨이]

away  away  away

---

| [ænt 앤트] | I love my aunt Amy. | 저는 Amy이모가 좋아요. |
| [ɔ́:təm 어–틈] | It is windy in the autumn. | 가을에는 바람이 많이 불어요. |
| [əwéi 어웨이] | Tom goes away. | Tom은 멀리 갔다. |

# Bb

**baby**
아기
[béibi 베이비]

baby  baby  baby

**back**
등, 뒤
[bæk 백]

back  back  back  back

**bad**
나쁜, 고약한
[bæd 배드]

bad  bad  bad  bad

**bag**
가방, 봉지
[bæg 백]

bag  bag  bag  bag

| [béibi 베이비] | The baby girl is my little sister. | 그 여자 아기는 내 여동생이에요, |
| [bæk 백] | I lddkxd his back. | 나는 그의 등을 보았어요, |
| [bæd 배드] | Thomas is a bad guy. | Thomas는 나쁜 사람이에요, |
| [bæg 백] | This is my schoolbag. | 이건 제 책가방이에요, |

## ball
공
[bɔːl 버-얼]

ball    ball    ball    ball

## balloon
풍선
[bəlúːn 벌루-운]

balloon    balloon

## banana
바나나
[bənǽnə 버내너]

banana    banana    banana

## band
끈, 묶는 것, 악단
[bænd 밴드]

band    band    band    band

## bank
은행
[bæŋk 뱅크]

bank    bank    bank    bank

| | | |
|---|---|---|
| [bɔːl 버-얼] | This is my sister's ball. | 이건 우리 누나의 공이에요. |
| [bəlúːn 벌루-운] | Tom's balloon is very big. | Tom의 풍선은 굉장히 커요. |
| [bənǽnə 버내너] | I like bananas very much. | 나는 바나나를 무척 좋아해요. |
| [bænd 밴드] | They are singing with the band. | 그들은 악단과 함께 노래를 하고 있다. |
| [bæŋk 뱅크] | My father work for that bank. | 우리 아빠는 저 은행에서 일하셔요. |

## base
토대, 기초

[beis 베이스]

base    base    base

## basket
바구니

[bǽskit 배스킷]

basket    basket    basket

## bath
목욕

[bæθ 배쓰]

bath    bath    bath

## be
~이다

[bi: 비-]

be   be   be   be   be   be

## beach
물가, 바닷가

[bi:tʃ 비-잇취]

beach   beach   beach

| | | |
|---|---|---|
| [beis 베이스] | The base of the statue is cement. | 그 조각상의 토대는 시멘트이다. |
| [bǽskit 배스킷] | What do you have in your basket? | 바구니 안에 뭐가 있어요? |
| [bæθ 배쓰] | Jenny likes to take a bath. | Jenny는 목욕하는 걸 좋아해요. |
| [bi: 비-] | He must be hungry. | 그는 배고픈게 틀림없어. |
| [bi:tʃ 비-잇취] | We will go to beach. | 우리는 바닷가에 갈 거예요. |

**bear** (1)
곰
[bɛər 베어-ㄹ]

bear    bear    bear

**bear** (2)
낳다
[bɛər 베어-ㄹ]

bear    bear    bear    bear

**beautiful**
아름다운
[bjúːtəfəl 뷰-러플]

beautiful    beautiful

**because**
왜냐하면
[bikɔ́ːz 비커-즈]

because    because

**become**
~이 되다
[bikʌ́m 비컴]

become    become

| | | |
|---|---|---|
| [bɛər 베어-ㄹ] | Bears like honey. | 곰은 꿀을 좋아해. |
| [bɛər 베어-ㄹ] | Dogs usually bear four puppies. | 개는 보통 4마리의 새끼를 낳는다. |
| [bjúːtəfəl 뷰-러플] | Snow White is beautiful. | 백설공주는 예뻐요. |
| [bikɔ́ːz 비커-즈] | I like Tom because he is kind. | 나는 Tom이 좋아요. 왜냐하면 친절하니까요. |
| [bikʌ́m 비컴] | Hungbu became the rich man. | 흥부는 부자가 되었어요. |

## bed
침대

[bed 뱃]

bed     bed     bed

## before
전에, 일찍이

[bifɔ́ːr 비포-어]

before     before     before

## begin
시작하다

[bigín 비긴]

begin     begin     begin

## behind
뒤에

[biháind 비하인드]

behind     behind     behind

## bell
종, 초인종

[bel 벨]

bell    bell    bell    bell

---

| | | |
|---|---|---|
| [bed 뱃] | We have three beds. | 우리는 침대가 3개 있어요. |
| [bifɔ́ːr 비포-어] | Spring comes before summer. | 여름이 오기 전에 봄이 옵니다. |
| [bigín 비긴] | Our class begins at 8. | 수업은 8시에 시작한다. |
| [biháind 비하인드] | Tom smiles behind Merry. | Tom은 Merry 뒤에서 미소 지었어요. |
| [bel 벨] | Listen! The bell is ringing. | 들어봐~ 종이 울리고 있어. |

**below**
~보다 아래에
[bilóu 빌로우]

below    below    below

**bench**
긴 의자, 벤치
[bentʃ 벤취]

bench    bench    bench

**beside**
~의 곁에
[bisáid 비싸이드]

beside    beside    beside

**best**
가장 좋은
[best 베스트]

best    best    best    best

**between**
~사이에
[bitwíːn 비트위-ㄴ]

between    between

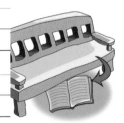

| | | |
|---|---|---|
| [bilóu 빌로우] | Cat is below the table. | 탁자 아래 고양이가 있어요. |
| [bentʃ 벤취] | There are three benches in the park | 공원에는 벤치가 3개 있다. |
| [bisáid 비싸이드] | Tom is standing beside his friends. | Tom은 친구들 옆에 서 있다. |
| [best 베스트] | I did my best. | 나는 최선을 다했어요. |
| [bitwíːn 비트위니] | Leave it between hat an hat. | 모자와 모자 사이에 그것을 놔두세요. |

## bicycle
자전거

[báisikəl바이시클]

bicycle    bicycle    bicycle

## big
큰, 커다란

[big 빅]

big    big    big    big

## bird
새

[bəːrd 버얼드]

bird    bird    bird    bird

## birthday
생일

[bɛ́ːrθdèi 벌쓰데이]

birthday    birthday    birthday

## black
검은 색

[blæk 블랙]

black    black    black    black

---

| [báisikəl바이시클] | Can you ride a bicycle? | 자전거를 탈 수 있나요? |
| [big 빅] | An elephant is a big animal. | 코끼리는 몸집이 큰 동물이에요, |
| [bəːrd 버얼드] | Birds fly in the air. | 새들은 공중을 날아다녀요, |
| [bɛ́ːrθdèi벌쓰데이] | When is your birthday? | 네 생일이 언제니? |
| [blæk 블랙] | The prince has black hair. | 왕자 머리카락은 검은색이에요, |

## blow
불다

[blou 블로우]

blow    blow    blow    blow

## blue
파란색

[blu: 블루-]

blue    blue    blue    blue

## board
판자, 게시판

[bɔːrd 보-르드]

board    board    board

## boat
보트, 작은배

[bout 보웃트]

boat    boat    boat    boat

## body
몸, 신체

[bádi 바디]

body    body    body

| | |
|---|---|
| [blou 블로우] | My father is blowing up balloons. |
| [blu: 블루-] | Jessica has blue eyes. |
| [bɔːrd 보-르드] | What's this new board for? |
| [bout 보웃트] | My uncle has a big boat. |
| [bádi 바디] | My whole body is aching now. |

아빠가 풍선을 불고 계셔요,
Jessica의 눈은 파란색이예요,
이 새 게시판은 어디에 쓸 거죠?
삼촌은 큰 보트를 가지고 계신다,
지금 온몸이 아파요,

## book
책

[buk 북]

book   book   book

## born
태어나다

[bɔːrn 보언]

born   born   born

## bottle
병

[bátl 바를]

bottle   bottle   bottle

## box
상자, 박스

[baks 박스]

box   box   box

## boy
소년

[bɔi 보이]

boy   boy   boy   boy

| | | |
|---|---|---|
| [buk 북] | Mom is reading a book for me. | 엄마가 저에게 책을 읽어주고 계세요. |
| [bɔːrn 보언] | I was born in Seoul. | 나는 서울에서 태어났다. |
| [bátl 바를] | There are many bottles in the shelf. | 선반에 병들이 많이 있어요. |
| [baks 박스] | I opened the box of chocolate. | 나는 초콜릿 상자를 열었어요. |
| [bɔi 보이] | Who is that boy? | 저 소년은 누구니? |

**bread**
빵
[bred 브레드]

bread    bread    bread

**break**
부수다
[breik브뢰익크]

break    break    break

**breakfast**
아침식사
[brékfəst 브뢰ㄱ퓌스트]

breakfast    breakfast

**bridge**
다리
[bridʒ 브륏쥐]

bridge    bridge

**bright**
밝은, 빛나는
[brait 브롸잇]

bright    bright    bright

| | | |
|---|---|---|
| [bred 브레드] | Tom, would ydu like some bread? | Tom, 빵 좀 먹을래? |
| [breik브뢰익크] | A glass is easy to break. | 유리는 깨지기 쉽다. |
| [brékfəst브뢰롓트] | I ate bread and milk for breakfast. | 나는 아침으로 빵과 우유를 먹었다. |
| [bridʒ 브륏쥐] | We walked across the bridge. | 우리는 걸어서 다리를 건넜어요. |
| [brait 브롸잇] | Look on the bright side of things. | 밝은 면을 봐(긍정적으로 생각하렴). |

**bring**
가져오다
[briŋ 브링]

bring    bring    bring

**broke**
깨트렸다
[brouk 브로-크]

broke    broke    broke

**broken**
부러진
[broukən 브뤄큰]

broken    broken    broken

**brother**
형제
[brʌðɔr 브롸덜]

brother    brother    brother

**brown**
갈색, 갈색의
[braun 브롸운]

brown    brown    brown

| | | |
|---|---|---|
| [briŋ 브링] | Bring me the book, please. | 그 책 좀 가져다 주렴. |
| [brouk 브로-크] | I broke my grandma's glasses. | 내가 할머니의 안경을 깨뜨렸다. |
| [broukən 브뤄큰] | My left arm was broken. | 내 왼쪽 팔이 부러졌다. |
| [brʌðɔr 브롸덜] | I have 2 younger brothers. | 어린 남동생(형제)이 두 명 있어요. |
| [braun 브롸운] | My teacher wears brown jacket. | 선생님은 갈색 자켓을 입고 계시다. |

23

## brush
붓, 손질하다
[brʌʃ 브러쉬]

brush    brush    brush

## build
세우다, 짓다
[bild 빌드]

build    build    build    build

## burn
타다, 태우다
[bəːrn 버-ㄹ언]

burn    burn    burn    burn

## bus
버스
[bʌs 버스]

bus    bus    bus    bus

## busy
바쁜
[bízi 비지]

busy    busy    busy    busy

---

[brʌʃ 브러쉬]      I brush my teeth clean everyday.      저는 매일 이를 깨끗하게 닦아요.

[bild 빌드]      I want to build my dog's house.      나는 개집을 짓고 싶어요.

[bəːrn 버-ㄹ언]      Mom burned the steaks today.      엄마는 오늘 스테이크를 태웠어요.

[bʌs 버스]      Look! Here comes a bus.      봐봐! 버스가 온다.

[bízi 비지]      My parents are busy.      우리 부모님은 바쁘셔요.

24

## but
그러나, 하지만

[bʌt 벗]

but   but   but   but

## butter
버터

[bʌ́tər 버러ㄹ]

butter   butter   butter

## button
단추, 버튼

[bʌ́tn 버튼]

button   button   button

| | | |
|---|---|---|
| [bʌt 벗] | He likes apples. But I don't. | 그는 사과를 좋아해요, 그러나 저는 안좋아해요. |
| [bʌ́tər 버러ㄹ] | There are bread and butter. | 빵과 버터가 있어요. |
| [bʌ́tn 버튼] | The baby is touching the buttons. | 아기가 단추를 만지고 있어요. |

## buy
사다, 구입하다

[bai 바이]

buy   buy   buy   buy

## by
곁에, ~로써

[bai 바이]

by   by   by   by   by   by

## bye
(헤어질 때)안녕

[bai 바이]

bye   bye   bye   bye

| | | |
|---|---|---|
| [bai 바이] | I buy some chocolate at the store. | 나는 가게에서 초콜릿을 삽니다, |
| [bai 바이] | I go to school by bus. | 나는 버스 타고(버스로) 학교가요, |
| [bai 바이] | "Good bye~ see you later." | "안녕~ 다음에 보자" |

## cake
케이크

[keik 케이크]

cake  cake  cake

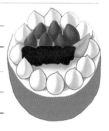

## calendar
달력

[kǽləndər캘린더-ㄹ]

calendar  calendar  calendar

## call
부르다

[kɔːl 커얼]

call  call  call  call  call

## came
왔다

[keim 케임]

came  came  came  came

| | | |
|---|---|---|
| [keik 케이크] | She gives ma a piece of cake. | 그녀는 나에게 케이크 한 조각을 주었다. |
| [kǽləndər캘린더-ㄹ] | There is a calendar on the wall. | 벽에 달력이 있어요. |
| [kɔːl 커얼] | My friends call me Sunny. | 친구들은 저를 Sunny라고 불러요. |
| [keim 케임] | Come to me plase. | 저에게 오세요. |

**camera**
카메라
[kǽmərə캐므러]

camera   camera   camera

**camp**
캠프
[kæmp 캠프]

camp   camp   camp

**can**
깡통
[kæn 캔]

can   can   can   can   can   ca

**candle**
양초
[kǽndl캔들]

candle   candle   candle

**candy**
사탕
[kǽndi 캔디]

candy   candy

| | | |
|---|---|---|
| [kǽmərə캐므러] | I want to buy a new digital camera. | 새 디지털카메라를 사고 싶어요. |
| [kæmp 캠프] | Let's go to camp. | 야영하러 가요. |
| [kæn 캔] | There are many empty cans. | 빈 깡통이 많이 있어요. |
| [kǽndl캔들] | That girl sells candles. | 저 소녀는 양초를 팔아요. |
| [kǽndi 캔디] | Andy gave me candy. | Andy가 나에게 사탕을 주었어요. |

## cap
모자

[kæp 캡]

cap cap cap cap

## capital
수도

[kǽpitl 캐피틀]

capital capital capital

## captain
선장, 우두머리

[kǽptin 캡틴]

captain captain captain

## car
자동차

[ka:r 카-ㄹ]

car car car car car car

## card
카드

[ka:rd카-ㄹ드]

card card card card card

| | | |
|---|---|---|
| [kæp 캡] | Mom bought me this cap. | 엄마가 이 모자를 사주셨어요. |
| [kǽpitl 캐피틀] | Seoul is the capital of Korea. | 서울은 대한민국의 수도에요. |
| [kǽptin 캡틴] | Mr. Han is the captain of the soccer team. | 한선생님은 그 축구팀의 주장이에요. |
| [ka:r 카-ㄹ] | Let's get into this car. | 이 차를 탑시다. |
| [ka:rd카-ㄹ드] | I sent him a birthday card. | 나는 그에게 생일 카드를 보냈어요. |

## care
조심, 주의

[kɛər 케어ㄹ]

care care care care

## careful
조심스러운

[kɛərfəl
캐어ㄹ풀]

careful careful

## carry
운반하다

[kǽri 캐뤼]

carry carry carry carry

## case
상자

[keis 케이쓰]

case case case case

## cassette
카세트

[kəsét 카세트]

cassette cassette cassette

---

| | | |
|---|---|---|
| [kɛər 케어ㄹ] | I don't care about that. | 난 그것에 대해 걱정하지 않아요. |
| [kɛərfəl캐어ㄹ풀] | Be careful not to drop the cup. | 컵을 떨어뜨리지 않게 조심해. |
| [kǽri 캐뤼] | I always carry schoolbag. | 저는 항상 책가방을 가지고 다녀요. |
| [keis 케이쓰] | Where is my glasses case? | 내 안경집(안경상자) 어디 있지? |
| [kəsét 카세트] | I need this cassette. | 노아는 이 카세트테이프가 필요해요. |

## cat
고양이

[kæt 캣]

cat   cat   cat   cat   cat

## catch
잡다, 받다

[kætʃ 캣취]

catch   catch   catch

## center
중앙, 중심

[séntər 쎈터ㄹ]

center   center   center

## chair
의자

[tʃɛər 췌어ㄹ]

chair   chair   chair

## chalk
분필

[tʃɔːk 초어크]

chalk   chalk   chalk

---

| | | |
|---|---|---|
| [kæt 캣] | I'm afraid of cats. | 저는 고양이가 무서워요. |
| [kætʃ 캣취] | Cats are very good at catching mice. | 고양이는 쥐를 아주 잘 잡아요. |
| [séntər 쎈터ㄹ] | Please, center the vase on the table. | 꽃병은 탁자 중앙에 두세요. |
| [tʃɛər 췌어ㄹ] | There is a cat under the chair. | 의자 밑에 고양이 한 마리가 있어요. |
| [tʃɔːk 초어크] | Let's buy blackboard and chalk. | 칠판과 분필을 삽시다. |

## chance
우연, 기회

[tʃæns 챈스]

chance   chance   chance

## change
변화

[tʃeindʒ 최인쥐]

change   change   change

## cheap
값이 싼, 싸게

[tʃiːp 취-입]

cheap   cheap   cheap

## cheese
치즈

[tʃiːz 취-즈]

cheese   cheese   cheese

## chicken
닭

[tʃikən 취킨]

chicken   chicken

| | | |
|---|---|---|
| [tʃæns 챈스] | It is a chance to meet him. | 그를 만날 기회이다. |
| [tʃeindʒ 최인쥐] | Let's change the subject. | 주제를 바꿉시다. |
| [tʃiːp 취-입] | The candy was very cheap. | 그 사탕은 값이 쌌어요. |
| [tʃiːz 취-즈] | Mice are eating cheese. | 쥐들이 치즈를 먹고 있어요. |
| [tʃikən 취킨] | The chickens make a lot of noise. | 닭들이 너무나 시끄럽게 해요. |

## child
어린이

[tʃaild 촤일드]

child     child     child

## children
child의 복수형

[tʃildrən 칠드런]

children    children    children

## church
교회

[tʃə:tʃ 춰-ㄹ취]

church     church     church

## circle
원, 동그라미

[sə́:rkl 써-ㄹ끌]

circle     circle     circle

## city
도시

[síti 씨리]

city    city    city    city

---

| | | |
|---|---|---|
| [tʃaild 촤일드] | The child always wishes to be a man. | 그 어린 아이는 항상 어른이 되기를 바래요. |
| [tʃildrən 칠드런] | There are a lot of children on the ground. | 운동장에 아이들이 많아요. |
| [tʃə:tʃ 춰-ㄹ취] | I go to church on Sundays. | 저는 일요일마다 교회에 가요. |
| [sə́:rkl 써-ㄹ끌] | He draw a circle on the paper. | 그가 종이에 원을 그렸어요. |
| [síti 씨리] | There are lots of people in the city. | 이 도시에는 사람들이 아주 많아요. |

## class
수업, 학급
[klæs 클래스]

class   class   class

## clean
깨끗한
[kli:n 클리인]

clean   clean   clean

## climb
오르다
[klaim 클라임]

climb   climb

## clock
시계
[klak 클락]

clock   clock   clock

## close(1)
닫다
[klouz클로우즈]

close   close   close

| [klæs 클래스] | It's time to finish the class. | 수업을 끝낼 시간이에요, |
| [kli:n 클리인] | I clean my room everyday. | 저는 제방을 매일 청소해요, |
| [klaim 클라임] | Mike climbs the mountain. | Mike는 산에 올라가요, |
| [klak 클락] | Tom broke his alarm clock. | Tom이 알람시계를 고장냈어요, |
| [klouz클로우즈] | Close one eye and look at that. | 한쪽 눈을 감고 저것을 봐봐, |

34

## close(2)
가까운, 친한

[klous클로우즈]

close     close     close

## clothes
옷

[klouðz클로우즈]

clothes     clothes

## cloud
구름

[klaud클라우드]

cloud     cloud     cloud

## club
클럽, 동호회

[klʌb 클럽]

club    club    club    club

## coat
외투

[kout 코웃]

coat   coat   coat   coat

---

| | | |
|---|---|---|
| [klous클로우즈] | Tom and Jerry are very close friends. | Tom과 Jerry는 아주 친한 친구 사이예요. |
| [klouðz클로우즈] | I'm making clothes for my cat. | 지금 제 고양이에게 입힐 옷을 만들고 있어요. |
| [klaud클라우드] | The birds fly over the clouds. | 새들이 구름 위로 날아다녀요. |
| [klʌb 클럽] | He is my club friend. | 그는 내 동호회 친구야. |
| [kout 코웃] | My grandfather bought me a blue coat. | 할아버지께서 파란색 코트를 사주셨어요. |

35

## coffee
커피

[kɔ́ːfi 커-퓌]

coffee   coffee   coffee

## coin
동전

[kɔin 코인]

coin  coin  coin  coin

## cold
추운

[kould 코울드]

cold  cold  cold

## color
색깔

[kʌ́lər 컬러ㄹ]

color  color  color  color

## come
오다

[kʌm 컴]

come  come  come

| | | |
|---|---|---|
| [kɔ́ːfi 커-퓌] | Give me a cup of coffee. | 커피 한 잔 주세요. |
| [kɔin 코인] | Put the coins into that machine. | 저 기계에 동전을 집어넣으세요. |
| [kould 코울드] | It is cold in January. | 1월에는 추워요. |
| [kʌ́lər 컬러ㄹ] | What is your favorite color? | 가장 좋아하는 색이 뭐야? |
| [kʌm 컴] | Grandfather will come next Friday. | 할아버지는 다음주 금요일날 오실꺼에요. |

36

**computer**
컴퓨터
[kəmpjú:tər
컴퓨-러ㄹ]

computer    computer

**cook**
요리사
[kúk 쿡]

cook    cook    cook    cook

**cool**
시원한
[ku:l 쿠울-]

cool    cool    cool    cool

**copy**
복사, 복사하다
[kápi 카피]

copy    copy    copy    copy

**corn**
옥수수
[kɔːrn 콘]

corn    corn    corn

---

[kəmpjú:tər컴퓨터ㄹ]    There are 3 computers on the desk.    책상위에 컴퓨터가 3대 있어요.
[kúk 쿡]    Mom cooks chickens for dinner.    엄마는 저녁 식사로 닭 요리를 하세요.
[ku:l 쿠울-]    It's cool.    시원하다.
[kápi 카피]    Please make a copy of this paper.    이 종이를 한 장만 복사해 주세요.
[kɔːrn 콘]    Do you like corn?    옥수수 좋아하세요?

**corner**
모퉁이

[kɔ́:rnər 코-널]

corner     corner     corner

**could**
can의 과거형

[kud 쿠드]

could     could

**count**
수를 세다

[kaunt 카운트]

count     count     count

**country**
나라, 지역

[kʌ́ntri 컨츠뤼]

country     country     country

**course**
진로, 과정

[kɔ:rs 코올스]

course     course     course

---

| [kɔ́:rnər 코-널] | Turn left at the corner. | 모퉁이에서 왼쪽으로 도세요. |
| [kud 쿠드] | I could carry the box. | 나는 그 상자를 옮길 수 있었어요. |
| [kaunt 카운트] | Let's count to 10! 1, 2, 3... | 10까지 세어보자! 일, 이, 삼... |
| [kʌ́ntri 컨츠뤼] | My grandmother lives in the country. | 할머니는 시골에서 사셔요. |
| [kɔ:rs코올스 ] | The full course is finished now. | 전 과정이 이제 끝났어요. |

## cousin
사촌, 친척

[kʌ́zn 커즌]

cousin    cousin    cousin

## cover
뚜껑

[kʌ́vər 커버-ㄹ]

cover    cover    cover

## cow
암소, 젖소

[kau 카우]

cow    cow    cow    cow

## crayon
크레용

[kréiən 크래이언]

crayon    crayon    crayon

## cream
크림

[kri:m 크뤼-임]

cream    cream

| | | |
|---|---|---|
| [kʌ́zn 커즌] | This is my cousin, Mike. | 얘는 내 사촌 Mike야. |
| [kʌ́vər 커버-ㄹ] | Snow covered the whole city. | 눈이 온 도시를 덮었다. |
| [kau 카우] | Cows make milk. | 암소들은 우유를 만들어요. |
| [kréiən 크래이언] | I like to draw lines using crayons. | 크래용으로 선긋는 것을 좋아해요. |
| [kri:m 크뤼-임] | Put two spoons of cream. | 크림 두 스푼을 넣으세요. |

## cross
가로지르다
[crɔːs 크러스]

cross    cross    cross

## cry
소리치다, 울다
[krai 크라이]

cry   cry   cry   cry   cry

## cucumber
오이
[kjúːkʌmbə 큐컴벌]

cucumber cucumber

## cup
컵
[kʌp 컵]

cup   cup   cup   cup

---

| | | |
|---|---|---|
| [crɔːs 크러스] | Let's cross the street. | 길을 건너자, |
| [krai 크라이] | "Why are you crying?" | 왜 울고 있니? |
| [kjúːkʌmbər 큐컴벌] | A cucumber is long and green. | 오이는 길고 녹색이다, |
| [kʌp 컵] | I bought this cup for mom. | 나는 엄마 드리려고 이 컵을 샀어요, |

## curtain
커튼

[kə́ːrtn 커튼]

curtain    curtain

## cut
베다, 깎다

[kʌt 컷]

cut   cut   cut    cut    cut

## cycle
순환, 한 바퀴

[sáikl 싸이클]

cycle   cycle   cycle   cycle

---

| | | |
|---|---|---|
| [kə́ːrtn 커튼] | I hide behind the curtain. | 전 커튼 뒤로 숨었어요. |
| [kʌt 컷] | I cut my finger. | 나는 손가락을 베었다. |
| [sáikl 싸이클] | It moves in a cycle. | 그것은 한 바퀴를 돌았어요. |

41

# Dd

| | |
|---|---|
| **dad/daddy**<br>아빠<br>[dæd 대드] | dad     dad     dad  |
| **dance**<br>춤, 춤추다<br>[dæns 댄스] | dance     dance     dance |
| **danger**<br>위험<br>[déindʒər 대인쥐ㄹ] | danger     danger     danger |
| **dark**<br>어둠, 어두운<br>[daːrk 다아-ㄹ크] | dark    dark    dark    dark |

| | | |
|---|---|---|
| [dæd 대드] | Dad reads me some books at night. | 아빠는 저에게 밤에 책을 읽어주셔요. |
| [dæns 댄스] | I like to dance. | 저는 춤추는 걸 좋아해요. |
| [déindʒər 대인쥐] | Look at that danger sign. | 저 위험 표시판을 보세요. |
| [daːrk 다아-ㄹ크] | My new skirt is dark blue. | 저의 새 치마는 어두운 파란색이예요. |

**date**
날짜
[deit 데잇트]

date　　date　　date　　date

**daughter**
딸
[dɔ́:tər 더-러]

daughter　daughter

**day**
낮, 하루
[dei 데이]

day　　day　　day　　day

**dead**
죽은
[ded 데드]

dead　　dead　　dead　　dead

**deep**
깊은
[di:p 디-입]

deep　　deep　　deep　　deep

---

| | | |
|---|---|---|
| [deit 데잇트] | What's the date today? | 오늘 몇일이에요?(오늘 날짜가 어떻게 되죠?) |
| [dɔ́:tər 더-러] | My aunt has 2 daughters and a son. | 우리 이모는 1남 2녀(아들한명과 두딸)를 두셨어요. |
| [dei 데이] | I play all day long every day. | 난 매일 하루 종일 놀아요. |
| [ded 데드] | My cat was dead. | 제 고양이가 죽었어요. |
| [di:p 디-입] | How deep is the river? | 강이 얼마나 깊나요? |

**deer**
사슴
[diər 디얼]

deer    deer    deer

**desk**
책상
[desk 데스크]

desk    desk    desk    desk

**dial**
다이얼
[dáiəl 다이얼]

dial    dial    dial    dial

**diary**
일기, 일기장
[dáiəri 다이어뤼]

diary    diary    diary    diary

**dictionary**
사전
[díkʃəneri 딕셔네뤼]

dictionary    dictionary

| | | |
|---|---|---|
| [diər 디얼] | Have you seen a deer? | 사슴을 본 적이 있니? |
| [desk 데스크] | There is a pencil on the desk. | 책상위에 연필 한 자루가 있어요. |
| [dáiəl 다이얼] | Sometimes I dial the wrong number. | 가끔 저는 틀린 번호로 전화를 걸어요. |
| [dáiəri 다이어뤼] | I don't feel like writing a diary now. | 나는 지금 일기 쓰고 싶지 않아요. |
| [díkʃəneri 딕셔네뤼] | Can I borrow your dictionary? | 당신의 사전을 빌릴 수 있을까요? |

## did
했다, 했었다
[did 디드]

did    did    did    did    did

## die
죽다
[dai 다이]

die    die    die    die    die

## dinner
저녁 식사
[dínər 디널]

dinner    dinner    dinner

## dirty
더러운, 불결한
[dʒːrti 더-ㄹ리]

dirty    dirty    dirty    dirty

## dish
접시
[diʃ 디쉬]

dish    dish    dish

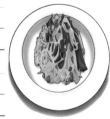

| | | |
|---|---|---|
| [did 디드] | I did a lot of things yesterday. | 어제 많은 일들을 했어요. |
| [dai 다이] | That sick dog will die. | 저 아픈 개는 죽을거야. |
| [dínər 디널] | I had dinner with my friend, Tony. | 나는 친구 Tony와 저녁을 먹었어요. |
| [dʒːrti 더-ㄹ리] | My brother's room is dirty all the time. | 내 동생 방은 항상 더러워요. |
| [diʃ 디쉬] | I help mom to wash the dishes. | 저는 엄마가 설거지하는 것을 도와드려요. |

## do
하다

[du: 드]

do　do　do　do　do　do

## does
do의 3인칭 단수

[dʌz 더즈]

does　does　does　does

## doctor
의사

[dɑ́ktər 닥터ㄹ]

doctor　doctor　doctor

## dog
개

[dɔːg 더-ㄱ]

dog　dog　dog

## doll
인형

[dal 덜]

doll　doll　doll　doll

| | | |
|---|---|---|
| [du: 드] | What did you do last weekend? | 지난 주에 뭐했니? |
| [dʌz 더즈] | What does she play? | 그녀는 무엇을 연주했니? |
| [dɑ́ktər 닥터ㄹ] | I would like to be a doctor. | 나는 의사가 되고 싶어요. |
| [dɔːg 더-ㄱ] | How many dogs are in the playground? | 운동장에 개가 몇 마리나 있나요? |
| [dal 덜] | Susan and I are playing with a doll. | Susan과 나는 인형놀이를 하고 있어요. |

**dollar**
달러

[dálər 달럴]

dollar dollar dollar

**door**
문

[dɔːr 도얼]

door door door

**down**
아래로

[daun 다운]

down down down

**dream**
꿈, 꿈을 꾸다

[driːm 드륌]

dream dream dream

**dress**
의복

[dres 드뢰스]

dress dress dress

| | | |
|---|---|---|
| [dálər달럴] | It's ten dollars. | 10달러입니다. |
| [dɔːr 도얼] | I knocked on the door. | 나는 문을 두드렸어요. |
| [daun 다운] | I went down the stairs. | 나는 계단을 내려갔어요. |
| [driːm 드륌] | In-ho had a dream last night. | 인호는 어젯밤에 꿈을 꾸었어요. |
| [dres 드뢰스] | I want to wear the pink dress. | 분홍색 드레스(옷)를 입고 싶어요. |

## drink
마시다

[driŋk 쥬륑크]

drink   drink   drink

## drive
운전하다

[draiv 드롸이브]

drive   drive   drive

## drop
떨어뜨리다

[drap 드롸ㅂ]

drop   drop   drop

## drum
북, 드럼

[drʌm 드럼]

drum   drum   drum

| | | |
|---|---|---|
| [driŋk 쥬륑크] | If you are thirsty, drink some water. | 목이 마르면 물을 좀 마시세요, |
| [draiv 드롸이브] | Can you drive a car? | 차 운전할 줄 알아요? |
| [drap 드롸ㅂ] | "Don't drop the dishes." | 접시 떨어뜨리지 마라, |
| [drʌm 드럼] | Peter is playing the drum. | Peter가 드럼을 치고 있어요, |

## dry
마른

[drai 드롸이]

dry　　　dry　　　dry　　　dry

## duck
오리

[dʌk 더-ㄱ]

duck　　duck　　duck　　duck

| | | |
|---|---|---|
| [drai 드롸이] | I dry the wet clothes. | 젖은 옷을 말려요. |
| [dʌk 더-ㄱ] | The ducks can't fly. | 오리는 날 수 없다. |

49

**ear**
귀

[iər 이얼]

ear    ear    ear    ear

**early**
이른, 일찍

[ə́:rli이-ㄹ리]

early   early   early   early

**earth**
지구, 땅

[ə́:rθ어-ㄹ쓰]

earth   earth   earth

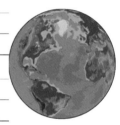

**east**
동쪽

[i:st 이스트]

east    east    east    east

| | | |
|---|---|---|
| [iər 이얼] | Rabbits have long ears. | 토끼의 귀는 길어요. |
| [ə́:rli어-ㄹ리] | I get up early in the morning. | 나는 아침 일찍 일어나요. |
| [ə́:rθ어-ㄹ쓰] | There are a lot of animals on the earth. | 지구에는 많은 동물들이 있어요. |
| [i:st 이스트] | Korea is to the east of China. | 한국은 중국 동쪽에 있다. |

## easy
쉬운
[íːzi 이–지]

easy  easy  easy  easy

## eat
먹다
[iːt 이–잇]

eat  eat  eat  eat

## egg
달걀
[eg 엑]

egg  egg  egg

## elephant
코끼리
[éləfənt 엘러풔ㄴ트]

elephant  elephant

## else
그밖에
[els 엘스]

else  else  else  else  else

| | | |
|---|---|---|
| [íːzi 이–지] | It's easy to say "Thank you." | 고맙다고 말하는 건 쉬워요. |
| [iːt 이–잇] | I like to eat salads. | 샐러드는 먹는 걸 좋아해요. |
| [eg 엑] | Chickens lay an egg each morning. | 닭은 매일 아침 달걀을 한 개씩 낳아요. |
| [éləfənt엘러풔ㄴ트] | The elephants are very strong. | 코끼리는 매우 힘이 세다. |
| [els 엘스] | "Anything else?" | 그 밖의 다른 것은요? |

## empty
텅 빈
[émpti 엠프티]

empty     empty

## end
끝, 마치다
[end 앤드]

end   end   end   end   end

## enjoy
즐기다
[éndʒɔ́i 엔줘이]

enjoy    enjoy    enjoy

## enough
충분한
[inʌ́f 이너프]

enough    enough    enough

## equal
같은
[íːkwəl 이퀴-얼]

equal    equal    equal

| | | |
|---|---|---|
| [émpti 엠프티] | The room is empty. | 그 방은 비었어요. |
| [end 앤드] | This is the end. | 이것으로 끝이다. |
| [éndʒɔ́i 엔줘이] | My dad enjoys driving. | 아빠는 운전을 즐기셔요. |
| [inʌ́f 이너프] | I think that's enough. | 그거면 충분하다고 생각해. |
| [íːkwəl 이퀴-얼] | Ducks are equal in size. | 오리들은 크기가 같다. |

**eraser**
지우개
[iréisər 이뢰이줘ㄹ]

eraser    eraser

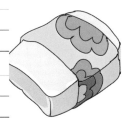

**evening**
저녁
[íːvniŋ이-브닝]

evening  evening   evening

**ever**
이제까지
[évər 에벌]

ever   ever    ever    ever

**every**
모든
[évriː에브뤼]

every     every     every

**example**
보기, 예
[igzǽmpl이그젬쁠]

example example  example

---

| | | |
|---|---|---|
| [iréisər이뢰이줘ㄹ] | Tom, can I borrow your eraser? | Tom, 지우개 좀 빌려줄래? |
| [íːvniŋ이-브닝] | It's windy this evening. | 오늘 저녁엔 바람이 분다. |
| [évər 에벌] | "Have you ever heard the song?" | 그 노래 들어봤니? |
| [évriː 에브뤼] | Everyone likes him. | 모두 그를 좋아해요. |
| [igzǽmpl이그젬쁠] | Can you give me an example? | 예를 하나 들어불래? |

**excite**
흥분시키다
[iksáit 익사잇트]

excite    excite    excite

**excuse**
용서하다
[ikskjú:z 익스큐즈]

excuse    excuse    excuse

**exercise**
운동, 연습
[éksərsáiz 엑썰싸이즈]

exercise  exercise  exercise

**eye**
눈
[ai 아이]

eye  eye  eye  eye

| | | |
|---|---|---|
| [iksáit 익사잇트] | The game excited us. | 그 시합은 우리를 흥분시켰다. |
| [ikskjú:z 익스큐즈] | Excuse me. | 실례합니다. |
| [éksərsáiz 엑썰싸이즈] | It's important to exercise everyday. | 매일 운동하는 것은 중요해요. |
| [ai 아이] | Open your eyes and look around. | 눈을 뜨고 주위를 둘러보세요. |

## face
얼굴

[feis푸ㅔ이스]

face   face   face   face

## fact
사실, 현실

[fækt 펙트]

fact   fact   fact   fact

## fair
공평한, 공정한

[fɛər 페얼]

fair   fair   fair   fair

## fall
가을

[fɔːl 풔ㄹ]

fall   fall   fall   fall

| | | |
|---|---|---|
| [feis푸ㅔ이스] | I wash my face everyday. | 나는 매일 얼굴을 씻어요(세수해요). |
| [fækt 펙트] | In fact, I don't like reading books. | 사실 전 독서를 좋아하진 않아요. |
| [fɛər 페얼] | I think it was a fair game. | 공정한 게임이었다고 생각해요. |
| [fɔːl 풔ㄹ] | In fall, we can see many leaves. | 가을에는 낙엽을 많이 볼 수 있어요. |

## family
가족

[fǽməli 페믈리]

family     family

## far
멀리

[faːr 퐈-ㄹ]

far far far far far far

## farm
농장

[faːrm 퐈-ㄹ암]

farm farm farm farm

## fast
빠른

[fæst 풰스트]

fast fast fast fast fast

## fat
뚱뚱한

[fæt 풰앳]

fat fat fat fat fat

---

| | | |
|---|---|---|
| [fǽməli 페믈리] | This is a picture of my family. | 우리 가족 사진이에요. |
| [faːr 퐈-ㄹ] | My house is far from here. | 우리집은 여기서 멀어요. |
| [faːrm 퐈-ㄹ암] | My grandfather works on this farm. | 할아버지는 이 농장에서 일하셔요. |
| [fæst 풰스트] | It is very fast train. | 이건 굉장히 빠른 기차에요. |
| [fæt 풰앳] | My cat is little fat, but very cute. | 우리 고양이는 조금 뚱뚱하지만 귀여워요. |

## father
아버지

[fá:ðər 퐈—덜]

father    father    father

## feel
느끼다

[fi:l 퓌—일]

feel    feel    feel    feel

## few
거의 없는

[fju: 퓨—]

few    few    few    few

## field
들판

[fi:ld 퓌—ㄹ드]

field    field    field

## fight
싸우다

[fait 퐈잇트]

fight    fight    fight    fight

| | | |
|---|---|---|
| [fá:ðər 퐈—덜] | I love my father. | 전 아빠를 사랑해요. |
| [fi:l 퓌—일] | I feel the summer is coming. | 여름이 오고있는게 느껴져요. |
| [fju: 퓨—] | I have few cards. | 나는 카드도 별로 없어요. |
| [fi:ld 퓌—ㄹ드] | The farmer works in the field. | 농부가 들판에서 일을 해요. |
| [fait 퐈잇트] | Sometimes I fight with my brother. | 가끔 동생이랑 싸워요. |

## fine
좋은

[fain 퐈인]

fine fine fine fine fine

## finger
손가락

[fiŋgər 휭거ㄹ]

finger finger finger

## fill
채우다

[fil 퓔]

fill fill fill fill fill fill fill fill

## film
필름, 영화

[film 필름]

film film film film

## find
찾다, 발견하다

[faind 퐈인드]

find find find find find

| | | |
|---|---|---|
| [fain 퐈인] | The weather is fine, today. | 오늘 날씨가 좋아요. |
| [fiŋgər 휭거ㄹ] | I touched water with my fingers. | 손가락으로 물을 만져보았어요. |
| [fil 퓔] | Fill in the blank. | 빈칸을 채우세요. |
| [film 필름] | My parents like to go to see a film. | 부모님은 영화보는 것을 좋아하세요. |
| [faind 퐈인드] | I can't find my doll. | 제 인형을 찾을 수가 없어요. |

**fire**
불
[faiər 파이얼]

fire fire fire fire fire

**finish**
끝내다, 마치다
[fíniʃ 휘니쉬]

finish finish finish finish

**fish**
물고기
[fiʃ 퓌쉬]

fish fish fish

**fix**
수리하다
[fiks 퓌ㄱ스]

fix fix fix fix fix fix

**flag**
기
[flæg 플래그]

flag flag flag flag

| | | |
|---|---|---|
| [faiər 파이얼] | I want to be a fire fighter. | 나는 소방관이 되고 싶어요. |
| [fíniʃ 휘니쉬] | Let's finish it today. | 오늘 그걸 끝냅시다. |
| [fiʃ 퓌쉬] | Did you catch any fish? | 고기 좀 잡으셨어요? |
| [fiks 퓌ㄱ스] | Dad and I will fix the roof today. | 아빠랑 오늘 지붕을 고칠꺼예요. |
| [flæg 플래그] | We made a flag today. | 우리는 오늘 깃발을 만들었어요. |

59

## floor
바닥, 층

[flɔːr 플로-월]

floor     floor     floor

## flower
꽃

[fláuər 플라워ㄹ]

flower     flower

## fly(1)
날다

[flai 플롸이]

fly   fly   fly   fly   fly   fly   fly

## fly(2)
파리

[flai 플롸이]

fly   fly   fly   fly   fly   fly   fly

## follow
따르다

[fálou 퐈ㄹ로우]

follow     follow     follow

---

| | | |
|---|---|---|
| [flɔːr 플로-월] | The book store is on the third floor. | 그 서점은 3층에 있어요, |
| [fláuər 플라워ㄹ] | A lily is one of my favorite flowers. | 백합은 제가 좋아하는 꽃 중에 하나에요, |
| [flai 플롸이] | I can't fly. | 나는 날 수 없어요, |
| [flai 플롸이] | Frog eats fly. | 개구리는 파리를 먹어요, |
| [fálou 퐈ㄹ로우] | "Where is the hospital?" "Follow me" | "병원이 어디있나요" "저를 따라오세요" |

60

**food**
음식
[fuːd 푸-드]

food    food    food

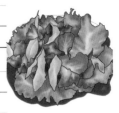

**fool**
바보
[fúːl 푸-울]

fool    fool    fool    fool    fool

**foolish**
어리석은
[fúːliʃ 푸-울리쉬]

foolish    foolish    foolish

**foot**
발
[fut 풋]

foot    foot    foot    foot    foot

**for**
~을 위해서
[fɔːr 포-ㄹ]

for for    for    for    for for for

| | | |
|---|---|---|
| [fuːd 푸-드] | What is your favorite food? | 좋아하는 음식은 무엇인가요? |
| [fúːl 푸-울] | Don't call your friend a fool. | 친구를 바보라고 부르지 마세요. |
| [fúːliʃ 푸-울리쉬] | It was a foolish idea. | 그건 어리석은 생각이었어요. |
| [fut 풋] | Peter is pushing the box with his foot. | Peter는 발로 상자를 밀고 있다. |
| [fɔːr 포-ㄹ] | This is for you. | 이것은 너를 위한 거야. |

## forget
잊다

[fərgét 폴겟]

forget　　forget　　forget

## fork
포크

[fɔːrk 포-ㄹ크]

fork　　fork　　fork

## form
모양, 형태

[fɔːrm 풔ㅁ]

form　　form　　form　　form

## free
자유로운

[friː 프뤼-]

free　　free　　free　　free

## fresh
새로운, 신선한

[freʃ 프뤳쉬]

fresh　　fresh　　fresh　　fresh

| | | |
|---|---|---|
| [fərgét 폴겟] | Did you forget to buy some apples? | 사과 사는 거 잊으셨어요? |
| [fɔːrk 포-ㄹ크] | Give me a fork and knife. | 제게 포크와 나이프를 주세요. |
| [fɔːrm 풔ㅁ] | Clouds have many different forms. | 구름은 여러 다양한 모양을 띤다. |
| [friː 프뤼-] | What do you do in your free time? | 한가할 때 뭐하세요? |
| [freʃ 프뤳쉬] | These vegetables looks fresh. | 이 야채들은 신선해 보여요. |

**four**
4, 4의
[fɔːr 포-]

four    four    four    four

**fox**
여우
[fɑks 팍스]

fox    fox    fox    fox

**friend**
친구
[frend프뤠ㄴ드]

friend    friend    friend

**from**
~에서
[frʌm 프럼]

from    from    from    from

| | | |
|---|---|---|
| [fɔːr 포-] | My family is four. | 우리가족은 4명입니다, |
| [fɑks팍스 ] | A fox is a wild animal. | 여우는 야생 동물이다, |
| [frend프뤠ㄴ드] | I have many friends. | 저는 친구가 많아요, |
| [frʌm 프럼] | I'm from Japan. | 저는 일본에서 왔어요, |

## front
앞
[frʌnt프뤄ㄴ트]

front    front    front    front

## fruit
과일
[fruːt푸룻-ㅌ]

fruit    fruit    fruit

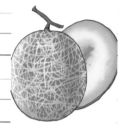

## full
가득한, 충만한
[ful 풀]

full   full   full   full   full

## fun
재미, 재미있는
[fʌn 풔ㄴ]

fun   fun   fun   fun   fun

---

| | | |
|---|---|---|
| [frʌnt프뤄ㄴ트] | I'll wait you at front door. | 앞 문에서 널 기다릴께, |
| [fruːt푸룻-ㅌ] | What is your favorite fruit? | 좋아하는 과일이 무엇인가요? |
| [ful 풀] | The box is full of books. | 이 박스에는 책이 가득 들어있다, |
| [fʌn 풔ㄴ] | It is fun to play the piano. | 피아노 치는건 재밌어요, |

## game
게임, 놀이
[geim 게임]

game　　game　　game

## garden
정원
[gá:rdn 가-ㄹ든]

garden　　garden

## gas
가스
[gæs 개스]

gas　　gas　　gas　　gas

## gate
문, 출입구
[geit 게잇트]

gate　　gate　　gate　　gate

---

| [geim 게임] | I like to play computer games. | 컴퓨터 게임 하는 거 좋아해요, |
| [gá:rdn 가-ㄹ든] | There are roses in that garden. | 저 정원엔 장미가 있어요, |
| [gæs 개스] | We field the ballon with gas. | 우리는 풍선에 가스를 채웠다, |
| [geit 게잇트] | There is a dog at the gate. | 문 앞에 개가 한 마리 있어요, |

## get
얻다, 받다

[get 겟]

get    get    get    get

## girl
소녀

[gə:rl 거얼]

girl    girl    girl    girl

## give
주다

[giv 기브]

give    give    give    give

## glad
기쁜, 반가운

[glæd 글래드]

glad    glad    glad    glad

## glass
유리, 유리컵

[glæs 글래쓰]

glass    glass    glass

| [get 겟] | How can I get to the church? | 교회까지 어떻게 가요? |
| [gə:rl 거얼] | That girl was wearing a blue skirt. | 그 소녀는 파란 치마를 입고 있었다. |
| [giv 기브] | Please, give me that book. | 저 책을 저에게 주세요. |
| [glæd 글래드] | I'm glad to meet you. | 만나서 반가워. |
| [glæs 글래쓰] | I drink three glasses of milk everyday. | 나는 매일 우유를 세 잔씩 마셔요. |

## glove
장갑
[glʌv 글러브]

glove glove glove

## go
가다
[gou 고우]

go go go go go go go

## god
하느님
[gad ]

god god god god god

## gold
금
[gould 고울드]

gold gold gold gold

## good
좋은, 착한
[gud 굿]

good good good good

| | | |
|---|---|---|
| [glʌv 글러브] | I left my gloves at home. | 내 장갑을 집에 두고 왔어요. |
| [gou 고우] | I go to school everyday. | 나는 매일 학교에 간다. |
| [gad 갓] | Oh, God. | 오, 신이시여. |
| [gould 고울드] | This box is full of gold. | 이 상자는 금으로 가득 차 있어요. |
| [gud 굿] | I think it is a good idea. | 좋은 생각인 것 같아요. |

**grandmother**
할머니

[grǽndmáːðər
그랜드머더]

grandmother    grandmother

**grape**
포도

[greip 그뢰입]

grape   grape   grape

**grass**
풀

[græs 그뢰쓰]

grass   grass    grass    grass

**gray**
회색, 회색의

[grei 그뢰이]

gray    gray    gray    gray

**great**
큰, 엄청난

[greit 그뤠잇]

great   great    great    great

| | | |
|---|---|---|
| [grǽndmáːðər 그랜드머더] | Grandmother likes to tell me funny story. | 할머니는 저에게 재밌는 얘기 해주시는 걸 좋아하셔요. |
| [greip 그뢰입] | Does Peter like grapes? | Peter는 포도를 좋아하나요? |
| [græs 그뢰쓰] | "Keep off the grass." | 잔디에 들어가지 마시오. |
| [grei그뢰이] | I like this gray sweater. | 나는 이 회색 스웨터가 좋아. |
| [greit 그뤠잇] | I heard some great news! | 나 엄청난 소식을 들었어! |

**green**
녹색
[gri:n 그뤼인]

green    green    green

**ground**
땅, 운동장
[graund그롸운드]

ground    ground

**group**
무리, 모임, 떼
[gru:p 구류웁]

group    group    group

**guitar**
기타
[gitá:r기타-ㄹ]

guitar    guitar    guitar

[gri:n 그뤼인]     I like green color.              저는 녹색을 좋아해요.
[graund그롸운드]   Let's play on the ground.        운동장에서 놀자.
[gru:p 구류웁]     Each group has its flag.         각 그룹마다 깃발이 있어요.
[gitá:r기타-ㄹ]    Can you play the guitar?         기타 칠 줄 아세요?

## hair
머리카락, 털

[hɛər 헤얼]

hair   hair   hair   hair

## half
반, 2분의1

[hæf 해프]

half   half   half   half

## hamburger
햄버거

[hǽmbəːrgər 햄버거]

hamburger    hamburger

## hand
손

[hænd 핸드]

hand   hand   hand

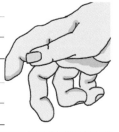

| | | |
|---|---|---|
| [hɛər 헤얼] | Koreans have a black hair. | 한국 사람의 머리카락은 검은 색이에요. |
| [hæf 해프] | Please cut this bread in half. | 이 빵을 반으로 잘라주세요. |
| [hǽmbəːrgər 햄버거] | Are you eating hamburger again? | 너 햄버거 또 먹는거야? |
| [hænd 핸드] | We must wash our hands. | 손을 꼭 씻어야 해요. |

70

## handle
손잡이

[hǽndl 핸들]

handle   handle   handle

## happen
발생하다

[hǽpən 햐푼]

happen  happen  happen

## happy
행복한

[hǽpi 해삐]

happy   happy   happy

## hard
딱딱한, 어려운

[haːrd 하알드]

hard   hard   hard   hard

## hat
모자

[hæt 햇]

hat  hat  hat  hat

| | | |
|---|---|---|
| [hǽndl 핸들] | Turn left this handle. | 이 손잡이를 왼쪽으로 돌리세요. |
| [hǽpən 햐푼] | How did it happen? | 어떻게 그 일이 발생했나요? |
| [hǽpi 해삐] | I'm happy to be with you. | 너랑 있어 행복해. |
| [haːrd 하알드] | It is very hard to solve this problem. | 이 문제를 해결하는 건 어려워요. |
| [hæt 햇] | Mrs. Lee always wears a hat. | 이 선생님은 항상 모자를 쓰고 다니셔요. |

71

| | |
|---|---|
| **hate**<br>싫어하다<br>[heit 헤잇트] | hate   hate   hate   hate |
| **have**<br>가지고 있다<br>[hæv 해브] | have   have   have   have |
| **he**<br>그는, 그가<br>[hi: 히-] | he he he he he he he |
| **head**<br>머리<br>[hed 헤드] | head  head  head |
| **hear**<br>듣다<br>[hiər 히얼] | hear  hear  hear  hear |

| | | |
|---|---|---|
| [heit 헤잇트] | I hate mouse. | 난 쥐를 싫어해. |
| [hæv 해브] | I have a lot of stamps. | 저는 우표를 아주 많이 가지고 있어요. |
| [hi: 히-] | He pointed the girl with a doll. | 그는 인형을 가지고 있는 그 소녀를 가르켰어요. |
| [hed 헤드] | His head touches the ceiling. | 그의 머리는 천장에 닿아요. |
| [hiər 히얼] | Can you hear me? | 내말 들리니? |

| **heart**<br>마음, 심장<br>[haːrt하-ㄹ트] | heart　heart　heart　heart |
| **heavy**<br>무거운<br>[hévi 헤뷔] | heavy　　heavy　　heavy |
| **hello**<br>안녕, 여보세요<br>[helóu 헬로우] | hello　hello　hello　hello |
| **help**<br>돕다<br>[help 헬-프] | help　help　help　help |
| **hen**<br>암탉<br>[hen 헨] | hen　hen　hen |

| | | |
|---|---|---|
| [haːrt하-ㄹ트] | The doctor is checking my heart. | 의사 선생님이 제 심장을 검사하고 계세요. |
| [hévi 헤뷔] | Elephants are really heavy. | 코끼리는 아주 무겁다. |
| [helóu 헬로우] | "Hello, may I speak to Tom?" | 여보세요, Tom이랑 통화할 수 있을까요? |
| [help 헬-프] | Help me, please! | 저를 도와주세요! |
| [hen 헨] | Hen lays an egg. | 암탉은 계란을 낳아요. |

**her**
그녀의
[hə:r 허-ㄹ]

her her her her

**here**
여기
[hiər 히얼]

here here here here

**hers**
그녀의 것
[hə:rz 허어즈]

hers hers hers hers

**herself**
그녀 자신
[hərsélf 허셀프]

herself herself herself

**hi**
안녕(만났을때)
[hai 하이]

hi hi hi hi hi hi hi hi hi

| | | |
|---|---|---|
| [hə:r 허-ㄹ] | Jane is doing her homework. | Jane은 숙제하고 있어요. |
| [hiər 히얼] | Han river is far from here. | 한강은 여기서 멀어요. |
| [hə:rz 허어즈] | This comic book is hers. | 이 만화책은 그녀의 것이야. |
| [hərsélf 허셀프] | She does it by herself. | 그녀는 그것을 그녀 자신이 했어요(혼자서 했어요). |
| [hai 하이] | Hi! I'm Jessica. Nice to meet you! | 안녕! 나는 Jessica야. 만나서 반가워! |

74

## hide
숨기다, 숨다
[haid 하이드]

hide　hide　hide　hide

## high
높은
[hái 하이]

high　high　high　high

## hill
언덕
[hil 힐]

hill　hill　hill　hill

## him
그를, 그에게
[him 힘]

him　him　him　him　him

## himself
그 자신
[himsélf 힘셀프]

himself　himself　himself

---

| | | |
|---|---|---|
| [haid 하이드] | Don't hide my doll. | 내 인형 숨기지마! |
| [hái 하이] | Mt. Everest is really high. | 에베레스트 산은 정말 높아요. |
| [hil 힐] | A cottage is on a hill. | 언덕 위에 작은집이 하나 있다. |
| [him 힘] | She loves him. | 그녀는 그를 사랑해요. |
| [himsélf 힘셀프] | "I can do it!", Ted told himself. | "할 수 있어!" Ted는 그 자신에게 말했습니다. |

## his
그의, 그의 것
[híz 히이스]

his his his his

## hit
때리다
[hit 힛]

hit hit hit hit hit hit

## hold
잡다, 붙들다
[hould 호울드]

hold hold hold hold

## hole
구멍
[houl 호울]

hole hole hole hole

## holiday
휴일, 공휴일
[hálədéi할러데이]

holiday holiday holiday

| | | |
|---|---|---|
| [híz 히이스] | This brown umbrella is his. | 이 갈색 우산은 그의 것이예요. |
| [hit 힛] | Don't hit me! | 나를 때리지 마. |
| [hould 호울드] | "Hold my hand!", he cries. | "내 손을 잡아!" 그가 외쳤어요. |
| [houl 호울] | "Peter, you have a hole in your pants." | Peter야 너 바지에 구멍 났어. |
| [hálədéi할러데이] | Did you have good holiday? | 휴일 잘 보내셨어요? |

76

**home**
집
[hóum 홈]

home     home

**hope**
바라다
[houp 호웁]

hope    hope    hope

**horse**
말
[hɔːrs 호올스]

horse    horse    horse

**hospital**
병원
[háspitl하스피틀]

hospital hospital hospital

**hot**
더운, 뜨거운
[hat 핫]

hot hot hot hot hot

---

[hóum 홈]
[houp 호웁]
[hɔːrs 호올스]
[háspitl하스피틀]
[hat 핫]

I have to stay home today.
I hope you have a good time.
Riding a horse is very funny.
Ted is in the hospital.
I don't like hot weather.

나는 오늘 집에 있어야만 해요.
좋은 시간되시길 바랍니다.
말타는 건 재밌어요.
Ted는 병원에 입원해 있어요.
나는 더운 날씨를 별로 안 좋아해요.

## hotel
호텔

[houtél 호텔]

hotel　hotel　hotel　hotel

## hour
시간

[auər 아우월]

hour　hour　hour

## house
집

[haus 하우스]

house　house　house

## how
어떻게, 얼마나

[hau 하우]

how　how　how　how

---

| [houtél 호텔] | How about staying in a hotel? | 호텔에 묵는 건 어때요? |
| [auər 아우월] | Peter slept for five hours. | Peter는 5시간동안 잤어요. |
| [haus 하우스] | There is a big house on the hill. | 언덕위에는 큰 집이 한 채 있어요. |
| [hau 하우] | How are you? | 어떻게 지내니? |

## hundred
백(100)

[hándrəd 헌드륏]

hundred   hundred   hundred

## hungry
배고픈

[hángri 헝그뤼]

hungry   hungry

## hurry
서두르다

[həːri 허-뤼]

hurry   hurry   hurry

## hurt
다치게 하다

[həːrt 허-르트]

hurt   hurt   hurt   hurt

---

[hándrəd 헌드륏]　My grandfather is one hundred years old.　할아버지는 100세이십니다.

[hángri 헝그뤼]　I'm very hungry.　나 정말 배고파요.

[həːri 허-뤼]　Hurry up! or we'll be late.　서둘러! 안 그러면 늦을꺼야.

[həːrt 허-르트]　I am badly hurt.　난 심하게 다쳤어요.

## I
나는, 내가

[ai 아이]

I I I I I I I I I I I I I I I I

## ice
얼음

[ais 아이스]

ice   ice   ice   ice

## idea
생각

[aidíːə아이디어]

idea idea idea idea idea

## if
(만약)~라면

[if 이프]

if if if if if if if if if if if if

| | | |
|---|---|---|
| [ai 아이] | I'm peter. I'm 10years old. | 나는 Peter예요, 10살이죠. |
| [ais 아이스] | I slipped on the ice. | 나는 얼음판에서 넘어졌어요. |
| [aidíːə아이디어] | Do you have any ideas? | 무슨 좋은 생각 있어? |
| [if 이프] | If I were you, I would do my best. | (만약)내가 너라면, 난 최선을 다할텐데. |

80

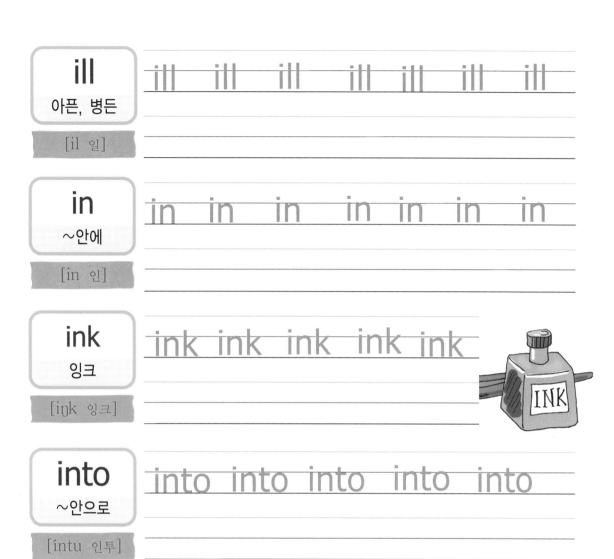

## ill
아픈, 병든

[il 일]

ill　ill　ill　ill　ill　ill　ill

## in
~안에

[in 인]

in　in　in　in　in　in　in

## ink
잉크

[iŋk 잉크]

ink ink　ink　ink ink

## into
~안으로

[íntu 인투]

into　into　into　into　into

| [il 일] | Teddy is ill in bed. | Teddy는 아파서 누워있어요. |
| [in 인] | There is a cat in the box. | 상자 안에 고양이 한 마리가 있다. |
| [iŋk 잉크] | Uncle is filling the pen with ink. | 삼촌이 펜에 잉크를 채워 넣고 계셔요. |
| [íntu 인투] | Jim goes into his house. | Jim은 그의 집으로 들어가요. |

## is
~에 있다

[íz 이즈]

is is is is is is is is is is

## island
섬

[áilənd아일런드]

island island

## it
그것은

[it 잇]

it it it it it it it it it it

---

[íz 이즈]     There is a cup of coffee on the table.     식탁위에 커피한잔이 있어요.

[áilənd아일런드]   I have never been to the island.     나는 그 섬에 가본 적이 없어요.

[it 잇]     It is your dog.     그것은 당신의 강아지예요.

# J j

## job
일, 직업

[dʒab 좝]

job job job job

## jump
뛰어오르다

[dʒʌmp 줘ㅁ프]

jump jump jump

## jungle
밀림, 정글

[dʒʌ́ŋgl 줘ㅇ글]

jungle jungle jungle

## just
방금, 오직

[dʒʌst 줘스트]

just just just just

| | | |
|---|---|---|
| [dʒab 좝] | "What's her job?" | 그녀의 직업은 무엇인가요? |
| [dʒʌmp 줘ㅁ프] | Teddy is ready to jump up. | Teddy는 뛰어오를 준비가 되었어요. |
| [dʒʌ́ŋgl 줘ㅇ글] | The lion is king of the jungle. | 사자는 밀림의 왕이에요. |
| [dʒʌst 줘스트] | I just arrived here. | 저는 방금 여기에 도착했어요. |

# K k

**keep**
계속하다
[ki:p 키-입]

keep   keep   keep   keep

**key**
열쇠
[ki: 키-]

key   key   key

**kick**
차다
[kik 킥]

kick   kick   kick   kick

**kill**
죽이다, 없애다
[kil 킬]

kill kill   kill   kill   kill

| | | |
|---|---|---|
| [ki:p 키-입] | Keep your room clean. | 당신의 방을 깨끗히 유지하세요, |
| [ki: 키-] | I lost my key yesterday. | 저는 어제 열쇠를 잃어버렸어요, |
| [kik 킥] | Tom kicks a ball. | Tom은 공을 차요, |
| [kil 킬] | Cats kill the mouse. | 고양이는 쥐를 죽여요, |

84

## kind
친절한

[kaind 카인드]

kind kind kind kind

## king
왕

[kiŋ 킹]

king king king

## kitchen
부엌

[kítʃin 킷췬]

kitchen kitchen kitchen

## knee
무릎

[ni: 니–]

knee knee knee knee

| | | |
|---|---|---|
| [kaind 카인드] | The police officer is very kind. | 그 경찰관은 매우 친절해요, |
| [kiŋ 킹] | The lion is the king of animals. | 사자는 동물의 왕이에요, |
| [kítʃin 킷췬] | Refrigerator is in the kitchen. | 냉장고는 부엌에 있어요, |
| [ni: 니–] | I feel pain in my knee. | 무릎이 아파요, |

## knife
칼
[naif 나이프]

knife   knife   knife

## knock
두드리다
[nak 낙]

knock   knock   knock

## know
알다, 이해하다
[nou 노우]

know   know   know

| [naif 나이프] | The knife is dangerous. | 그 칼은 위험해요. |
| [nak 낙] | I knocked the door. | 전 노크를 했어요. |
| [nou 노우] | Do you know what I mean? | 내가 무슨 말 하는 지 알겠어? |

## lady
숙녀, 부인

[léidi 레이디]

lady　lady　lady　lady

## lake
호수

[leik 레익]

lake　lake　lake

## lamp
등불

[læmp 램프]

lamp　lamp　lamp　lamp

## land
땅, 육지

[lænd 랜드]

land　land　land　land

| | | |
|---|---|---|
| [léidi 레이디] | The lady over there is my aunt. | 저기있는 숙녀분은 우리 고모에요. |
| [leik 레익] | There are many lakes in Canada. | 캐나다에는 호수가 많아요. |
| [læmp 램프] | I use my desk lamp when I study. | 저는 공부할 때 책상램프를 사용해요. |
| [lænd 랜드] | Everyone seems to have more lands. | 모든 사람들은 더 많은 땅을 원하는 것 같아요. |

## large
큰
[lɑːrdʒ 라-ㄹ쥐]

large    large    large

## last
마지막
[læst 래스트]

last    last    last    last    last

## late
늦은, 늦게
[leit 레잇]

late    late    late    late    last

## laugh
웃다
[læf 래프]

laugh    laugh    laugh

## lead
인도하다
[liːd 리드]

lead    lead    lead    lead

| | | |
|---|---|---|
| [lɑːrdʒ 라-ㄹ쥐] | I want large size skirt. | 전 큰 사이즈 치마를 원해요. |
| [læst 래스트] | When did you see him last? | 마지막으로 그를 본 게 언제였죠? |
| [leit 레잇] | Let's meet at 7 o'clock. Don't be late. | 7시에 만나자, 늦지마! |
| [læf 래프] | He laughs loudly. | 그는 큰 소리로 웃었어요. |
| [liːd 리드] | Lead him to the place. | 그를 그 장소로 인도하시오. |

## leaf
나뭇잎
[liːf 리-프]

leaf     leaf     leaf     leaf

## learn
배우다
[ləːrn 러-ㄹ언]

learn    learn    learn    learn

## leave
떠나다
[liːv 리-브]

leave    leave    leave    leave

## left
왼쪽, 왼쪽의
[left 레프트]

left    left    left    left    left

## leg
다리
[leg 렉]

leg    leg    leg    leg

| | | |
|---|---|---|
| [liːf 리-프] | Look! The red leaf is falling. | 봐봐! 빨간 나뭇잎이 떨어지고 있어, |
| [ləːrn 러-ㄹ언] | I want to learn English. | 전 영어를 배우고 싶어요, |
| [liːv 리-브] | I leave at 3. | 나는 3시에 떠나요, |
| [left 레프트] | Turn left there. | 저기서 왼쪽으로 도세요, |
| [leg 렉] | I broke my leg three days ago. | 3일전에 다리가 부러졌어요,, |

## lesson
수업

[lésn 렛쓴]

lesson    lesson

## let
시키다

[let 렛]

let let let let let let

## letter
편지

[létər 레러-ㄹ]

letter    letter    letter

## library
도서관

[láibreri 라이브뢰뤼]

library    library    library

## lie(1)
눕다

[lai 라이]

lie lie lie lie lie lie

| | | |
|---|---|---|
| [lésn 렛쓴] | I have no lesson today. | 오늘은 수업이 하나도 없어요. |
| [let 렛] | I let him go out. | 그를 나가게 했어요. |
| [létər 레러-ㄹ] | I send a letter to my friend Min-su. | 나는 친구 민수에게 편지를 보내요. |
| [láibreri 라이브뢰뤼] | Mom and I often go to a library. | 엄마랑 저는 가끔 도서관에 가요. |
| [lai 라이] | Children lie on the bed. | 아이들이 침대에 누워요. |

## lie(2)
거짓말

[lai 라이]

lie lie lie lie lie lie

## life
생명, 생활

[lɑif 라이프]

life life life life

## light(1)
가벼운

[lait 라잇트]

light light light

## light(2)
빛, 조명

[lait 라잇트]

light light light light

lie

## like(1)
좋아하다

[laik 라이크]

like like like like

| | | |
|---|---|---|
| [lai 라이] | He tells a lie a lot. | 그는 거짓말을 많이 해요. |
| [lɑif 라이프] | Thank you for saving my life. | 제 생명을 구해주셔서 감사해요. |
| [lait 라잇트] | Tom is lighter than his brother. | Tom은 그의 형보다 가벼워요. |
| [lait 라잇트] | Don't forget to turn off the light. | 불(조명)끄는 것 잊지 마! |
| [laik 라이크] | I like dancing. | 저는 춤추는 걸 좋아해요. |

91

## like(2)
~와 닮은

[laik 라이크]

like   like   like   like   like

## line
선

[lain 라인]

line   line   line   line   line

## lion
사자

[láiən 라이언]

lion   lion   lion   lion

## lip
입술

[lip 립]

lip  lip  lip  lip  lip  lip  lip

## listen
듣다

[lísn 리슨]

listen  listen  listen  listen

| [laik 라이크] | Tom looks like his father. | Tom은 그의 아빠를 닮았어요. |
| [lain 라인] | Please, draw a line on the paper. | 종이에 선을 그리세요. |
| [láiən 라이언] | A lion found a zebra. | 사자가 얼룩말을 발견했어요. |
| [lip 립] | Sunny has a full lips. | Sunny는 입술이 두꺼워요. |
| [lísn 리슨 ] | I listen to the music everyday. | 나는 매일 음악을 듣는다. |

## little
작은
[litl 리를]

little    little    little

## live
살다
[liv 리브]

live    live    live    live

## lonely
외로운
[lóunli 로ㄴ리]

lonely  lonely  lonely   lonely

## long
긴
[lɔːŋ 러-엉]

long    long    long    long

## look
보다
[luk 룩]

look    look    look    look

| | | |
|---|---|---|
| [litl 리를] | Tom is walking with the little boy. | Tom이 작은 소년과 걷고 있어요. |
| [liv 리브] | Where do you live? | 사시는 곳이 어디에요? |
| [lóunli 로ㄴ리] | I feel lonely. | 나는 외롭다. |
| [lɔːŋ 러-엉] | A giraffe has a long neck. | 기린은 목이 길어요. |
| [luk 룩] | Look at it. Do you know what it is? | 이것 좀 봐, 이게 뭔지 알어? |

**lose**
잃다
[lu:z 루즈]

lose　lose　lose　lose

**lot**
많음
[lat 랏]

lot  lot  lot  lot  lot

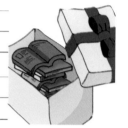

**loud**
목소리가 큰
[laud 라우드]

loud  loud  loud  loud  loud

**love**
사랑하다
[lʌv 러브]

love  love  love  love  love

| [lu:z 루즈] | Don't lose the key. | 열쇠 잃어버리지 마. |
| [lat 랏] | There are a lot of people on the beach. | 해변에 사람이 많아요. |
| [laud 라우드] | He has a loud voice. | 그는 목소리가 커요. |
| [lʌv 러브] | Mom and dad love each other. | 엄마 아빠는 서로를 사랑하셔요. |

**low**
낮은
[lou 로우]

low    low    low    low

**luck**
행운
[lʌk 럭]

luck    luck    luck

**lunch**
점심
[lʌntʃ런취]

lunch lunch lunch lunch

| | | |
|---|---|---|
| [lou 로우] | Dad has a low voice. | 아빠의 목소리는 좀 낮아요, |
| [lʌk 럭] | Good luck! | 행운을 빌어요 |
| [lʌntʃ런취] | It's time for lunch. | 점심 먹을 시간이에요, |

# Mm

**ma'am**
아주머니
[mæm 맴]

ma'am    ma'am    ma'am

**mad**
미친, 열광한
[mæd 매드]

mad    mad    mad    mad

**mail**
우편
[meil 메일]

mail    mail    mail

**make**
만들다
[meik 메이크]

make    make    make    make

| | | |
|---|---|---|
| [mæm 맴] | -Min-ho. -Yes, ma'am. | 민호야, 예, 선생님. |
| [mæd 매드] | He is mad about games. | 그는 게임에 열중해 있다. |
| [meil 메일] | I send a letter by mail. | 나는 편지를 우편으로 보낸다. |
| [meik 메이크] | I made a cake for my mother. | 나는 어머니를 위해 케이크를 만들었어요. |

**man**
남자
[mæn 맨]

man     man     man

**many**
많은
[méni 매니]

many     many     many

**map**
지도
[mæp 맵]

map     map     map

**march**
행진
[maːrtʃ 마-ㄹ취]

march     march     march

**market**
시장
[máːrkit 마-ㄹ킷]

market     market     market

| [mæn 맨] | The man is my father. | 그 남자는 나의 아버지예요. |
| [méni 매니] | He has many friends. | 그는 친구들이 많아요. |
| [mæp 맵] | I marked my house on the map. | 우리(나의) 집을 지도에 표시했다. |
| [maːrtʃ 마-ㄹ취] | Solders march along the street. | 군인들이 길을 따라 행진해요. |
| [máːrkit 마-ㄹ킷] | I will buy apples at market. | 시장에서 사과를 살 거예요. |

97

## marry
결혼하다

[mǽri 매뤼]

marry  marry   marry

## matter
문제, 곤란

[mǽtər 매터]

matter matter  matter

## may
~해도 좋다

[mei 메이]

may  may   may   may

## me
나를

[mi 미-]

me  me  me  me  me

## meat
고기

[miːt 미-잇트]

meat meat  meat

| | | |
|---|---|---|
| [mǽri 매뤼] | He will marry a woderful woman. | 그는 멋진 여성과 결혼할 것이다. |
| [mǽtər 매터] | What is the matter with you? | 무슨 일이야? |
| [mei 메이] | You may go now. | 넌 이제 가도 좋다. |
| [mi 미-] | Look at me! | 나를 보세요. |
| [miːt 미-잇트] | We will have meat for dinner. | 우리는 저녁식사로 고기를 먹을 거야. |

**meet**
만나다
[miːt 미잇트]

meet meet meet meet

**men**
man의 복수형
[men 멘]

men men men men

**mice**
mouse의 복수형
[mɑís 마이스]

mice mice mice mice

**middle**
중간, 한가운데
[mídl 미들]

middle middle middle

**milk**
우유
[milk 밀크]

milk milk milk

| [miːt 미잇트] | I am glad to meet you. | 만나게 되어서 기뻐요. |
| [men 멘] | Most men like playing football. | 대부분의 남자들은 축구하는 것을 좋아한다. |
| [mɑís 마이스] | Mice like cheeses. | 쥐들은 치즈를 좋아한다. |
| [mídl 미들] | He is a middle school student. | 그는 중학생이다. |
| [milk 밀크] | Milk is good for our health. | 우유는 건강에 좋다. |

**million**
100만

[míljən 밀리언]

million million million

**mine**
나의 것

[máin 마인]

mine mine mine mine

**minute**
분

[mínit 미닛]

minute minute minute

**mirror**
거울

[mírər 미뤄-ㄹ]

mirror mirror

**Miss**
~양, 선생님

[mis 미스]

Miss Miss Miss Miss

| | | |
|---|---|---|
| [míljən 밀리언] | He has one million won. | 그는 백만원이 있어요. |
| [máin 마인] | The pen is mine. | 그 펜은 내거야. |
| [mínit 미닛] | We have only 5 minutes. | 우리는 오직 5분의 시간이 없어(우리는 5분밖에 시간이 없어) |
| [mírər 미뤄-ㄹ] | She stands before a mirror all day. | 그녀는 하루 종일 거울 앞에 서 있다. |
| [mis 미스] | Miss Marry works hard. | Marry 양은 열심히 일을 한다. |

**mom**
엄마
[mam 맘]

mom   mom   mom

**money**
돈
[mʌ́ni 머니]

money   money   money

**monkey**
원숭이
[mʌ́ŋki 멍끼]

monkey  monkey  monkey

**month**
달
[mʌnθ 먼쓰]

month   month   month

**moon**
달
[mu:n 무-ㄴ]

moon  moon  moon

| | | |
|---|---|---|
| [mam 맘] | Mom got angry with me. | 어머니가 나에게 화가 나셨다. |
| [mʌ́ni 머니] | How much money do you have? | 넌 돈이 얼마 있니? |
| [mʌ́ŋki 멍끼] | Monkeys like bananas. | 원숭이들은 바나나를 좋아해요. |
| [mʌnθ 먼쓰] | I go to movies once a month. | 나는 한 달에 한번 영화를 보러 가요. |
| [mu:n 무-ㄴ] | There is a moon. | 달이 떴다. |

**morning**
아침
[mɔ́ːrniŋ 모-ㄹ닝]

morning     morning

**mother**
어머니
[mʌ́ðər 머덜]

mother   mother   mother

**mountain**
산
[mauntən마운튼]

mountain    mountain

**mouth**
입
[mauθ 마웃쓰]

mouth     mouth

**move**
움직이다
[muːv 무-ㅂ]

move   move   move

| | | |
|---|---|---|
| [mɔ́ːrniŋ모-ㄹ닝] | Good morning! | 좋은 아침! |
| [mʌ́ðər 머덜] | She is my mother. | 그녀는 나의 어머니예요. |
| [mauntən마운튼] | I climbed a mountain last Saturday. | 나는 지난 토요일 산에 올랐어요. |
| [mauθ 마웃쓰] | Tom opened his mouth. | Tom은 입을 벌렸어요. |
| [muːv 무-ㅂ] | We moved a new house. | 우리는 새집으로 이사했어요. |

**movie**
영화
[múːvi 무-뷔]

movie     movie

**Mr.**
~씨, 선생님
[místər 미스떠ㄹ]

Mr.   Mr.   Mr.   Mr.   Mr.   Mr.

**Mrs.**
~부인
[mísiz 미씨즈]

Mrs.   Mrs.   Mrs.   Mrs.   Mrs.

**much**
많은
[mʌtʃ 멋취]

much    much    much

---

| | | |
|---|---|---|
| [múːvi 무-뷔] | I went to the movie with my friends. | 나는 친구들과 영화를 보러 갔다. |
| [místər 미스떠ㄹ] | Mr. Kim is reading a paper. | 김 선생님은 신문을 읽고 계신다. |
| [mísiz 미씨즈] | Mrs. Smith washes the dishes. | 스미스 부인은 설거지를 한다. |
| [mʌtʃ 멋취] | Don't spend too much money. | 돈을 너무 많이 쓰지 마세요. |

**music**
음악
[mjú:zik 뮤-직]

music music music music

**must**
꼭 해야만 한다
[mʌst 머스트]

must must must must

**my**
나의
[maí 마이]

my my my my

| | | |
|---|---|---|
| [mjú:zik 뮤-직] | I like listening to music. | 나는 음악 듣는 것을 좋아한다. |
| [mʌst 머스트] | You must do this. | 당신은 이것을 해야만 한다. |
| [maí 마이] | This is my digital camera. | 이것은 제 디지털카메라예요. |

## name
이름

[neim 네임]

name name name name

## near
가까운

[niər 니얼]

near near near near

## neck
목

[nek 넥]

neck neck neck

## need
필요하다

[ni:d 니-드]

need need need need

| | | |
|---|---|---|
| [neim 네임] | What's your name? | 네 이름이 뭐니? |
| [niər 니얼] | Our house stands near my school. | 우리집은 학교 옆에 있어요. |
| [nek 넥] | A neck is a part of our body. | 목은 우리몸의 한 부분이다. |
| [ni:d 니-드] | I need an umbrella. | 나는 우산이 필요해요. |

## new
새로운

[nju: 뉴-]

new    new    new    new

## news
소식

[nju:z 뉴-즈]

news news news news

## next
다음의, 다음에

[nekst 넥스트]

next    next    next    next

## nice
멋진

[nais 나이스]

nice    nice    nice    nice

## night
밤

[nait 나잇]

night night night

| | | |
|---|---|---|
| [nju: 뉴-] | I wear a new uniform. | 나는 새로운 교복을 입는다, |
| [nju:z 뉴-즈] | Did you hear the news? | 그 소식 들었어? |
| [nekst 넥스트] | I like this best and that next. | 이것이 가장 마음에 들고 다음은 저것이다, |
| [nais 나이스] | This jacket is very nice. | 이 자켓은 매우 멋져요, |
| [nait 나잇] | I stayed up all night. | 나는 밤새도록 깨어 있었다, |

## no
하나도 없는

[nóu 노우]

no no no no no no no no

## noon
정오, 한 낮

[nuːn 눈]

noon noon noon noon

## north
북쪽

[nɔːrθ 노-ㄹ쓰]

north north north north

## nose
코

[nouz 노우즈]

nose nose nose

| | | |
|---|---|---|
| [nóu 노우] | There are no one in the room. | 방엔 아무도 없어요, |
| [nuːn 눈] | We have lunch at noon. | 우리는 정오에 점심을 먹는다, |
| [nɔːrθ 노-ㄹ쓰] | My house stands in the north of Seoul. | 우리 집은 서울의 북쪽에 있다, |
| [nouz 노우즈] | We have a nose. | 우리는 하나의 코를 가지고 있다, |

## not
아니다, 않다

[nat 낫]

not not not not

## now
지금, 방금

[nau 나우]

now now now now now

## number
수, 숫자

[nʌ́mbər 넘벌]

number number number

## nurse
간호사

[nəːrs 널쓰]

nurse nurse nurse

---

| [nat 낫] | Is it a cat? No, It is not. | 그것은 고양이입니다? 그것은 고양이가 아닙니다. |
| [nau 나우] | It is over now. | 이제 끝났다. |
| [nʌ́mbər 넘벌] | The number is two. | 그 숫자는 2이다. |
| [nəːrs 널쓰] | She is a nurse. | 그녀는 간호사이다. |

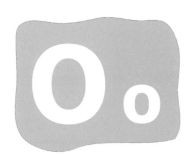

## Oo

**o'clock**
~시(정각)
[əklák 어클락]

o'clock  o'clock  o'clock

**of**
~의, ~중에서
[əv 어브]

of  of  of  of  of  of  of  of

**off**
~떨어져
[ɔːf 어프]

off  off  off  off  off  off  off

**office**
사무실
[ɔ́ːfis어-퓌스]

office  office  office

| | | |
|---|---|---|
| [əklák 어클락] | It is 6 o'clock. | 6시예요, |
| [əv 어브] | One of my friends likes apples. | 내 친구들 중 한명은 사과를 좋아한다, |
| [ɔːf 어프] | Don't take off your shoes. | 신발 벗지 마세요, |
| [ɔ́ːfis어-퓌스] | He works hard in his office. | 그는 그의 사무실에서 열심히 일한다, |

109

**often**
자주, 종종
[ɔ́ːfən 어-픈]

often often often often

**oh**
오~, 앗, 아~!
[ou 오우]

oh oh oh oh oh oh oh

**oil**
기름
[ɔ́il 오일]

oil oil oil oil oil

**OK**
좋다
[óukéi오우케이]

ok ok ok ok ok ok ok

**old**
늙은
[ould 오울드]

old old old old old old old

| | | |
|---|---|---|
| [ɔ́ːfən 어-픈] | How often do you go to the movie? | 얼마나 자주 영화 보러 가요? |
| [ou 오우] | Oh, no! | 오, 이런! |
| [ɔ́il 오일] | We need more oil. | 우리에겐 기름이 더 필요해요. |
| [óukei오우케이] | That's ok. | 괜찮아. |
| [ould 오울드] | How old are you? | 몇 살이지요? |

## on
~의 위에

[an 언]

on on on on on on on

## only
오직, 유일한

[óunli 오운리]

only only only only

## open
열다

[óupən 오우쁜]

open open open

## or
또는

[ɔːr 오-얼]

or or or or or or or or

| | | |
|---|---|---|
| [an 언] | My pencil is on the desk. | 책상 위에 내 연필이 있어요. |
| [óunli 오운리] | She is an only daughter. | 그녀는 외동딸이야. |
| [óupən 오우쁜] | Open the door, please. | 문좀 열어 주세요. |
| [ɔːr 오-얼] | Do you want this or that? | 이걸 원하세요, 또는 저걸 원하세요? |

**orange**
오렌지 색

[ɔ́ːrindʒ오륀쥐]

orange    orange    orange

**our**
우리의

[auər 아우월]

our  our   our    our

**ours**
우리의 것

[auərz아워즈]

ours   ours   ours   ours  ours

**out**
밖으로, 밖에

[aut 아웃]

out    out    out    out    out

---

| [ɔ́ːrindʒ오륀쥐] | Where is my orange shirt? | 내 오렌지색 셔츠 어디있니? |
| [auər 아우월] | That buildings is our school. | 저 건물이 우리 학교야. |
| [auərz아워즈] | Ours is a large family. | 우리 가족은 대 가족이야. |
| [aut 아웃] | Let's go out. | 우리 밖으로 나가자. |

## Pp

**page**
페이지, 쪽

[peidʒ 페이쥐]

page page page page

**paint**
페인트

[peint 페인트]

paint paint paint

**pair**
한쌍

[pɛ̀ər 페얼]

pair pair pair pair

**pants**
바지

[pænts 팬츠]

pants pants pants pants

| | | |
|---|---|---|
| [peidʒ 페이쥐] | Open your page 6. | 6쪽을 펴세요. |
| [peint 페인트] | Pass me that can of paint, please. | 그 페인트통 좀 건네줘요. |
| [pɛ̀ər 페얼] | Mom bought me a pair of shoes. | 엄마가 저에게 구두 한 켤레를 사주셨어요. |
| [pænts 팬츠] | I wear pants. | 나는 바지를 입는다 |

| | | |
|---|---|---|
| **paper**<br>종이<br>[péipər페이펄] | paper   paper | 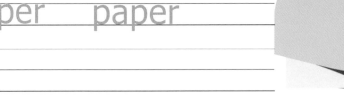 |
| **pardon**<br>용서, 용서하다<br>[páːrdn파-ㄹ든] | pardon  pardon  pardon | |
| **parent**<br>부모님<br>[pɛ́ərənt페어뤄ㄴ트] | parent  parent  parent | |
| **park**<br>공원<br>[paːrk파-ㄹ크] | park park  park  park | |
| **party**<br>파티, 모임<br>[páːrti파-ㄹ리] | party party party  party | |

| | | |
|---|---|---|
| [péipər페이펄] | I need a sheet of paper. | 종이 한 장이 필요하다, |
| [páːrdn파-ㄹ든] | I beg your pardon. | 죄송합니다, |
| [pɛ́ərənt페어뤄ㄴ트] | My parents are very nice. | 나의 부모님은 매우 좋으신 분이에요, |
| [paːrk파-ㄹ크] | We met in the park last night. | 우리는 지난밤 공원에서 만났어요, |
| [páːrti파-ㄹ리] | Can you come to my party | 내 파티에 올래? |

**pass**
지나가다
[pæs 패스]

pass  pass  pass  pass

**pay**
지불하다
[pei 페이]

pay  pay  pay  pay

**peace**
평화
[piːs 피―스]

peace  peace  peace

**pear**
(과일)배
[pɛər 페얼]

pear  pear  pear

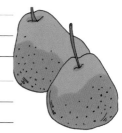

**pen**
펜
[pen 펜]

pen  pen  pen  pen

| | | |
|---|---|---|
| [pæs 패스] | I passed through the park. | 나는 공원을 가로질러 지나갔다. |
| [pei 페이] | We pay the school expenses. | 우리는 학비를 낸다. |
| [piːs 피―스] | I want world peace. | 나는 세계 평화를 원한다. |
| [pɛər 페얼] | This pear is sweet. | 이 배는 달다. |
| [pen 펜] | Can I borrow your pen? | 내가 네 펜을 빌릴 수 있을까? 혹은 펜좀 빌려줄래? |

| | | |
|---|---|---|
| **pencil**<br>연필<br>[pénsəl 펜쓸] | pencil　　pencil | |
| **people**<br>사람들, 국민<br>[píːpl 피-쁠] | people　people　people | |
| **piano**<br>피아노<br>[piǽnou 피애노우] | piano　piano　piano | |
| **pick**<br>따다<br>[pik 픽] | pick pick　pick　pick | |
| **picnic**<br>소풍<br>[píknik 피크닉] | picnic　picnic　picnic | |

| | | |
|---|---|---|
| [pénsəl 펜쓸] | Do you have pencils? | 너 연필 있니? |
| [píːpl 피-쁠] | People like flowers. | 사람들은 꽃을 좋아해요. |
| [piǽnou 피애노우] | I can play the piano. | 나는 피아노 연주를 할 수 있어요. |
| [pik 픽] | Please, pick one of them. | 그것들 중 하나를 고르세요. |
| [píknik 피크닉] | We went on a picnic last weekend. | 우리는 지난 주말에 소풍을 갔다. |

## picture
그림, 사진
[píktʃər 픽춰얼]

picture    picture    picture

## piece
조각, 단편
[píːs 피-스]

piece    piece    piece

## pig
돼지
[pig 픽]

pig    pig    pig    pig

## pilot
조종사
[páilət 파일럿]

pilot    pilot    pilot    pilot

## pin
핀
[pin 핀]

pin    pin    pin    pin    pin

---

| | | |
|---|---|---|
| [píktʃər 픽춰얼] | The picture hangs on the wall. | 그 사진은 벽에 걸려 있다. |
| [píːs 피-스] | I ate a piece of cake. | 나는 케이크 한 조각을 먹었다. |
| [pig 픽] | Pigs eat a lot. | 돼지는 많이 먹어요. |
| [páilət 파일럿] | I want to be a pilot. | 나는 조종사가 되고 싶어요. |
| [pin 핀] | Please, lend me a safety pin. | 안전핀 좀 빌려주세요. |

**pink**
분홍
[piŋk 핑크]

pink    pink    pink    pink

**place**
장소, 곳
[pleis플레이스]

place   place   place   place

**plan**
계획, 계획하다
[plæn 프랜]

plan    plan    plan    plan

**plane**
비행기
[plein 플레인]

plane   plane   plane   plane

**plant**
식물
[plænt 플랜트]

plant   plant   plant

| | |
|---|---|
| [piŋk 핑크] | I like the color of pink. |
| [pleis플레이스] | The place is very nice. |
| [plæn 프랜] | What is your next plan? |
| [plein 플레인] | Have you ever taken an air plane? |
| [plænt 플랜트] | The plants need water. |

나는 분홍색을 좋아해요.
그 장소는 매우 멋져.
당신의 다음 계획은 뭐예요?
비행기 타 본 적 있니?
식물은 물이 필요하다.

## play
연주하다, 놀다

[plei 플레이]

play play play play

## please
기쁘게 하다

[pliːz 플리이즈]

please please please

## pocket
호주머니

[pάkit 파킷]

pocket pocket pocket

## point
요점, 끝

[pɔint 포인트]

point point point point

## police
경찰

[pəlíːs 펄리-스]

police police police

| | | |
|---|---|---|
| [plei 플레이] | She plays the violin very well. | 그녀는 바이올린 연주를 매우 잘한다. |
| [pliːz 플리이즈] | I am pleased to see you. | 너를 보게 되어 기뻐. |
| [[pάkit 파킷] | She put her hand in her pockets. | 그녀는 주머니에 손을 넣었어요. |
| [pɔint 포인트] | The point of this pen is sharp. | 이 펜의 끝은 날카롭다. |
| [pəlíːs 펄리-스] | Police caught a thief. | 경찰이 도둑을 잡았어요. |

## pool
웅덩이, 연못
[pu:l 푸-울]

pool   pool   pool   pool

## poor
가난한, 불쌍한
[puə*r* 푸얼]

poor   poor   poor

## present
선물, 현재
[pré znt프뤼즌트]

present   present   present

## pretty
귀여운, 예쁜
[príti 프뤼티]

pretty   pretty   pretty

---

| [pu:l 푸-울] | Fish are in the pool. | 연못에 물고기들이 있어요, |
| [puə*r* 푸얼] | He is a poor man. | 그는 불쌍한 사람이다, |
| [pré znt프뤼즌트] | What is your present? | 네 선물은 뭐니? |
| [príti 프뤼티] | She is very pretty. | 그녀는 너무 귀여워요, |

**pull**
당기다
[pul 풀]

pull   pull   pull

**push**
밀다
[puʃ 푸쉬]

push  push  push  push

**put**
놓다, 두다
[put 풋]

put  put  put  put  put

| | | |
|---|---|---|
| [pul 풀] | Pull the door open. | 문을 당겨서 열어요. |
| [puʃ 푸쉬] | Push the door open. | 문을 밀어서 열어요. |
| [put 풋] | I put some flowers into the vase. | 꽃병에 꽃 몇 송이를 넣었다. |

# Qq

| | |
|---|---|
| **queen**<br>여왕<br>[kwiːn 퀴이-ㄴ] | queen    queen    queen |
| **question**<br>질문<br>[kwéstʃən 퀘스천] | question    question  |
| **quick**<br>빠른<br>[kwik 퀵] | quick   quick   quick   quick |
| **quiet**<br>조용한<br>[kwáiət 콰이엇-ㅌ] | quiet   quiet   quiet   quiet |

| | | |
|---|---|---|
| [kwiːn 퀴이-ㄴ] | A queen is the wife of a king. | 여왕은 왕의 아내이다. |
| [kwéstʃən 퀘스천] | Please answer my question. | 질문에 대답해 주세요. |
| [kwik 퀵] | He is quick to learn. | 그는 배우는 속도가 빠르다. |
| [kwáiət 콰이엇-ㅌ] | Be quiet! | 조용히 해! |

## radio
라디오

[réidióu뢰이디오]

radio  radio  radio

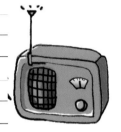

## rain
비, 비가오다

[rein 뢰인]

rain    rain    rain    rain

## rainbow
무지개

[réinbóu뢰인보우]

rainbow    rainbow    rainbow

## ran
달렸다

[ræn 랜]

ran  ran  ran  ran  ran

| | | |
|---|---|---|
| [réidióu뢰이디오] | I often listen to the radio. | 나는 종종 라디오를 듣는다, |
| [rein 뢰인] | I walked in the rain. | 나는 빗속을 걸었어요, |
| [réinbóu뢰인보우-] | We can see a rainbow. | 무지개가 뜬다, |
| [ræn 랜] | Tiger ran fast. | 오랑이는 빨리 달렸다, |

**read**
읽다, 낭독하다
[riːd 뤼-드]

read read read read

**ready**
준비가 된
[rédi 뢰디]

ready ready ready ready

**real**
현실의, 진짜의
[ríːəl 뤼-얼]

real real real real real

**really**
정말로
[ríəli 뤼얼리]

really really really

**record**
기록하다
[rikɔ́ːrd뢰커-르드]

record record record

| | | |
|---|---|---|
| [riːd 뤼-드] | I read a book loudly. | 나는 책을 큰소리로 읽었다. |
| [rédi 뢰디] | Are you ready to order? | 주문할 준비 되셨어요? |
| [ríːəl 뤼-얼] | This is a real story. | 이 이야기는 실재하는 이야기다. |
| [ríəli 뤼얼리] | I really like him. | 나는 그를 정말 좋아해요. |
| [rikɔ́ːrd뢰커-르드] | I record everything in this note. | 나는 모든 것을 이 노트에 기록한다. |

## red
빨간색, 붉은
[red 뢰드]

red red red red

## remember
기억하다
[rimémbər 뤼멤버얼]

remember remember

## rest
휴식
[rest 뤠스트]

rest rest rest rest rest

## restaurant
레스토랑
[réstərənt뢰스토뤈트]

restaurant restaurant

## ribbon
리본
[ríbən 뤼번]

ribbon ribbon ribbon

| | | |
|---|---|---|
| [red 뢰드] | She was red with shame. | 그녀는 부끄러워서 얼굴이 빨개졌다. |
| [rimémbər뤼멤버얼] | I remember her. | 나는 그녀를 기억한다. |
| [rest 뤠스트] | Take a rest. | 휴식을 취하세요. |
| [réstərənt뢰스토뤈트] | We had a dinner at restaurant. | 우리는 레스토랑에서 저녁을 먹었어요. |
| [ríbən 뤼번] | She wears red ribbon on her hair. | 그녀는 머리에 빨간 리본을 하고 있다. |

## rice
쌀. 밥

[rais 롸이스]

rice  rice  rice  rice

## rich
돈 많은

[ritʃ 륏취]

rich  rich  rich  rich

## ride
타다

[raid 롸이드]

ride  ride  ride  ride

## right
오른쪽

rait 롸잇트]

right  right  right

## ring(1)
울리다

[riŋ 륑]

ring  ring  ring  ring

| | | |
|---|---|---|
| [rais 롸이스] | Korean usually eat rice. | .한국 사람들은 보통 밥을 먹는다. |
| [ritʃ 륏취] | He is very rich. | 그는 매우 부유하다. |
| [raid 롸이드] | Can you ride a bicycle? | 자전거 탈 줄 아니? |
| rait 롸잇트] | Turn right. | 오른쪽으로 도세요. |
| [riŋ 륑] | The telephone is ringing. | 전화가 울리고 있어요. |

## ring (2)
반지

[riŋ 링]

ring   ring   ring   ring

## river
강

[rívər 뤼버-ㄹ]

river   river   river

## road
길, 도로

[roud 로우드]

road   road   road   road

## robot
로봇

[roubɔt 롸벗]

robot   robot   robot   robot

## rocket
로켓

[rákit 롸킷]

rocket   rocket   rocket

| | | |
|---|---|---|
| [riŋ 링] | He gave me a ring. | 그가 나에게 반지를 주었어요. |
| [rívər 뤼버-ㄹ] | I jumped into the river. | 나는 강에 뛰어 들었어요. |
| [roud 로우드] | The road is narrow. | 그 도로는 좁아요. |
| [roubɔt 롸벗] | My dad gave me a robot. | 아버지께서 로봇을 사 주셨어요. |
| [rákit 롸킷] | The rocket launched last Friday. | 그 로켓은 지난 금요일 발사되었다. |

**roof**
지붕
[ruːf 루-프]

roof　　roof　　roof　　roof

**room**
방
[ruːm 루-움]

room　　room　　room　　room

**rose**
장미
[rouz 로우즈]

rose　　rose　　rose

**round**
둥근, 동그란
[raund 롸운드]

round　　　round　　　round

**run**
달리다
[rʌn 뤄ㄴ]

run　　run　　run　　run　　run

| [ruːf 루-프] | Our house has a red roof. | 우리집에는 빨간 지붕이 있다. |
| [ruːm 루-움] | I study in my room. | 나는 내 방에서 공부해요. |
| [rouz 로우즈] | The red rose is beautiful. | 그 빨간 장미는 아름답다. |
| [raund 롸운드] | There is a round table. | 거기 둥근 탁자가 있다. |
| [rʌn 뤄ㄴ] | I like to run. | 나는 달리는 걸 좋아해요. |

## S s

**sad**
슬픈, 슬퍼하는

[sæd 쌔드]

sad   sad   sad   sad

**safe**
안전한

[seif 쎄이프]

safe   safe   safe   safe

**salad**
샐러드

[sǽləd 쌜러드]

salad   salad   salad

**salt**
소금

[sɔːlt 써-얼트]

salt   salt   salt   salt

| | | |
|---|---|---|
| [sæd 쌔드] | I am very sad. | 나는 매우 슬퍼요. |
| [seif 쎄이프] | There is a safe place. | 안전한 장소다. |
| [sǽləd 쌜러드] | I ate some salad and chicken. | 나는 샐러드와 치킨을 먹었다. |
| [sɔːlt 써-얼트] | Could you pass me the salt, please. | 소금 좀 건내 주시겠어요? |

| sand 모래 | sand sand sand |
| [sænd 쌘드] | |

| say 말하다 | say say say say |
| [sei 세이] | |

| school 학교, 수업 | school school school |
| [sku:l 스꾸-울] | |

| score 점수 | score score score |
| [skɔːr 스코어-ㄹ] | |

| sea 바다 | sea sea sea sea |
| [siː 씨-] | |

| [sænd 쌘드] | We built sand castles. | 우리는 모래성을 쌓았다. |
|---|---|---|
| [sei 세이] | Don't say no. | 안 된다고 말하지 마세요. |
| [sku:l 스꾸-울] | After school, I came back home. | 수업이 끝난 후, 나는 집으로 돌아 왔어요. |
| [skɔːr 스코어-ㄹ] | I got high score. | 난 높은 점수를 받았어요. |
| [siː 씨-] | I went to the sea last summer. | 나는 지난 여름에 바다에 갔어요. |

| | |
|---|---|
| **season**<br>계절<br>[síːzn 씨-즌] | season    season    season |
| **seat**<br>자리, 좌석<br>[síːt 씨-잇트] | seat   seat   seat   seat |
| **see**<br>보다<br>[síː 씨-] | see    see    see    see |
| **sell**<br>팔다<br>[sel 쎌] | sell sell sell sell  |
| **send**<br>보내다<br>[send 쎈드] | send    send    send |

| | | |
|---|---|---|
| [síːzn 씨-즌] | What's your favorite season? | 가장 좋아하는 계절은? |
| [síːt 씨-잇트] | Please, have a seat. | 앉으세요, |
| [síː 씨-] | I want to see you! | 네가 보고싶어 |
| [sel 쎌] | He sells cars. | 그는 자동차를 판다, |
| [send 쎈드] | I will send you an e-mail. | 나는 너에게 e-mail을 보낼 것이다, |

131

## set
한 벌, 짝, 세트
[set 세엣]

set    set    set    set

## shall
~일 것이다
[ʃæl 쉐엘]

shall    shall    shall

## shape
모양, 형태
[ʃeip 세입]

shape    shape    shape

## she
그녀는, 그녀가
[ʃi: 쉬]

she    she    she    she

## sheep
양
[ʃi:p 쉽]

sheep    sheep

| | | |
|---|---|---|
| [set 세엣] | I have a set of gloves. | 나는 장갑 한 쌍이 있다. |
| [ʃæl 쉐엘] | I shall be very happy to see you. | 너를 보게 되면 매우 기쁠 거야. |
| [ʃeip 세입] | The shape of a ball is round. | 그 공의 모양은 둥글다. |
| [ʃi: 쉬] | She is really beautiful. | 그녀는 정말 아름다워요. |
| [ʃi:p 쉽] | I have never seen sheep. | 나는 양을 본 적이 없어요. |

**sheet**
시트, 한 장
[ʃi:t 쉬-잇트]

sheet   sheet   sheet

**ship**
배
[ʃip 쉽]

ship   ship   ship

**shirt**
셔츠
[ʃəːrt 셔-ㄹ츠]

shirt   shirt   shirt

**shoe**
신, 구두
[ʃu: 슈-]

shoe   shoe   shoe

**shoot**
쏘다, 던지다
[ʃuːt 슈-웃]

shoot   shoot   shoot

| | | |
|---|---|---|
| [ʃi:t 쉬-잇트] | Please, give me three sheet of paper. | 제게 종이 3장을 주세요. |
| [ʃip 쉽] | Look at that ship! | 저 배를 봐요! |
| [ʃəːrt 셔-ㄹ츠] | I bought this shirt last year. | 작년에 이 셔츠를 샀어요. |
| [ʃu: 슈-] | My father bought a pair of shoes for me. | 아빠가 저에게 신발(한켤레)을 사주셨어요. |
| [ʃuːt 슈-웃] | He tried to shoot a bird. | 그는 새 한 마리를 쏘려고 하였다. |

**shop**
가게
[ʃap 샵]

shop   shop   shop

**short**
짧은, 키가작은
[ʃɔːrt 쇼-르트]

short   short   short

**shout**
소리치다
[ʃaut 샤웃]

shout   shout   shout

**show**
보이다
[ʃou 쇼우]

show   show   show

**shower**
소나기, 샤워
[ʃáuər 샤우월]

shower   shower

---

| | | |
|---|---|---|
| [ʃap 샵] | I went to the toy shop. | 나는 장난감가게로 갔다. |
| [ʃɔːrt 쇼-르트] | She is shorter than me. | 그녀는 나보다 더 작아요. |
| [ʃaut 샤웃] | Don't shout to your brother. | 동생에게 소리치지 마라. |
| [ʃou 쇼우] | Can you show it to me? | 그것을 내게 보여줄 수 있니? |
| [ʃáuər 샤우월] | I took a shower, today. | 나는 오늘 샤워했어요. |

## shut
닫다, 덮다
[ʃʌt 셧]

shut　　shut　　shut

## sick
아픈, 병든
[sik 씩]

sick　　sick　　sick

## side
옆, 면, 편
[said 싸이드]

side　　side　　side

## sign
기호, 서명하다
[sain 싸인]

sign　　sign　　sign

## silver
은, 은빛, 은의
[sílvər 씰뷔얼]

silver silver silver

| [ʃʌt 셧] | Please shut the window. | 창문 좀 닫아 주세요, |
| [sik 씩] | My grandmother is sick. | 할머니가 아프시다, |
| [said 싸이드] | Min-ho took our side. | 민호는 우리 편에 들었다, |
| [sain 싸인] | He signed the bill. | 그는 영수증에 서명하였다, |
| [sílvər 씰뷔얼] | He gave me a silver ring. | 그는 나에게 은반지를 주었다, |

**sing**
노래, 노래하다

sing    sing    sing

**sister**
여자형제, 언니

[sístər 씨스털]

sister    sister    sister

**sit**
앉다

[sit 씻]

sit    sit    sit    sit    sit

**size**
크기

[saiz 사이즈]

size    size    size    size

**skate**
스케이트

[skeit스케잇-트]

skate    skate    skate

| | | |
|---|---|---|
| [siŋ 씽] | My hobby is to sing songs. | 내 취미는 노래 부르는 것이다. |
| [sístər 씨스털] | I have two sisters. | 나는 두 명의 여자형제가 있어요. |
| [sit 씻] | Sit down, please. | 앉아 주세요. |
| [saiz 사이즈] | The size of the cap is too big. | 그 모자의 크기는 너무 크다. |
| [skeit스케잇-트] | Let's go skating! | 스케이트 타러가자! |

## skirt
스커트
[skə:rt스꺼얼트]

skirt    skirt    skirt

## sky
하늘
[skai 스까이]

sky  sky  sky  sky

## sled
썰매
[sled 스레드]

sled    sled    sled

## sleep
잠자다
[sli:p슬리-입]

sleep    sleep    sleep

## slide
미끄러지다
[slaid슬라이드]

slide    slide    slide

---

| | | |
|---|---|---|
| [skə:rt스꺼얼트] | She wears a skirt. | 그녀는 치마를 입고 있다. |
| [skai 스까이] | Look at the blue sky! | 저 파란 하늘을 봐! |
| [sled 스레드] | In winter, we sled. | 겨울에 우리는 썰매를 탄다. |
| [sli:p슬리-입] | I went to sleep at 9 o'clock. | 나는 9시에 잤어요. |
| [slaid슬라이드] | She slid on the ice. | 그녀는 얼음판 위에서 미끄러졌다. |

## slow
느린
[slou 슬로우]

slow     slow     slow

## slowly
천천히
[slóulí슬로울리]

slowly     slowly     slowly

## small
작은
[smɔːl스모-ㄹ]

small    small    small

## smell
냄새맡다
[smel 스멜]

smell     smell     smell

## smile
웃다, 미소지다
[smail 스마일]

smile     smile     smile

| | | |
|---|---|---|
| [slou 슬로우] | The turtle is slow. | 거북이는 느리다, |
| [slóulí슬로울리] | Could you speak more slowly? | 조금 더 천천이 말씀해 주시겠어요? |
| [smɔːl스모-ㄹ] | The ball is small. | 그 공은 작다, |
| [smel 스멜] | It smells good. | 좋은 냄새가 난다, |
| [smail 스마일] | She smiled at me. | 그녀가 나를 보고 웃었다, |

**smoke**
(담배)연기
[smouk스목ㅋ]

smoke   smoke   smoke

**snow**
눈, 눈이오다
[snou 스노우]

snow   snow   snow

**so**
정말로, 그렇게
[sou 쏘우]

so  so  so  so  so  so

**soap**
비누
[soup 쏘웁]

soap   soap   soap

**soccer**
축구
[sákər 싸커ㄹ]

soccer   soccer   soccer

| | | |
|---|---|---|
| [smouk스목ㅋ] | I hate cigarette smoke. | 나는 담배 연기가 싫어요. |
| [snou 스노우] | It is snowing. | 눈이 오고 있다. |
| [sou 쏘우] | You must not behave so. | 그렇게 행동해서는 안된다. |
| [soup 쏘웁] | Wash your hand with soap. | 비누로 손을 깨끗이 씻어라. |
| [sákər 싸커ㄹ] | I played soccer with my friends. | 나는 친구들과 축구를 했어요. |

## sock
양말
[sak 싹]

sock   sock   sock

## sofa
소파
[sóufə 쏘우풔]

sofa   sofa   sofa

## some
얼마간의, 다소
[sʌm 썸]

some   some   some

## son
아들
[sʌn 썬]

son   son   son

## song
노래
[sɔːŋ 썽]

song   song   song

| | | |
|---|---|---|
| [sak 싹] | I'm looking for my red socks. | 나는 내 빨간 양말을 찾고 있다. |
| [sóufə 쏘우풔] | The cushion is on the sofa. | 그 쿠션은 소파 위에 있다. |
| [sʌm 썸] | I bought some flowers. | 나는 꽃을 좀 샀다. |
| [sʌn 썬] | He is my son. | 그는 나의 아들이다. |
| [sɔːŋ 썽] | I sang a song for my parents. | 나는 부모님을 위해 노래를 불렀어요. |

**soon**
곧
[suːn 쑤-운]

soon　　soon　　soon

**sorry**
죄송한
[sɔ́ːri 써-뤼]

sorry　　sorry　　sorry

**sound**
소리
[sáund싸운드]

sound　　sound　　sound

**soup**
수프
[suːp 쑤웊]

soup　　soup　　soup

**south**
남쪽
[sauθ싸웃쓰]

south　south　south

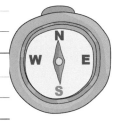

| | | |
|---|---|---|
| [suːn 쑤-운] | See you soon. | 곧 보자! |
| [[sɔ́ːri 써-뤼] | I am sorry to hear that. | 그것 참 유감이에요. |
| [sáund싸운드] | I heard some strange sound. | 나 이상한 소리를 들었어. |
| [suːp 쑤웊] | I made soup for you. | 너를 위해서 수프를 만들었어. |
| [sauθ싸웃쓰] | The man went south. | 그는 남쪽으로 갔다. |

**space**
공간, 우주
[speis스뻬이스]

space　　space

**speak**
말하다
[spi:k스뻭-ㅋ]

speak　　speak　　speak

**speed**
속력, 빠르기
[spid스뻬-드]

speed　　speed　　speed

**spell**
철자
[spel 스뻴]

spell　　spell　　spell

**spend**
낭비하다
[spend 스뻰드]

spend　　spend　　spend

| | | |
|---|---|---|
| [speis스뻬이스] | The people are looking for a parking space. | 사람들이 주차할 공간을 찾고 있다. |
| [spi:k스뻭-ㅋ] | I can speak English. | 나는 영어를 말할 수 있어요.\ |
| [spid스뻬-드] | He ran with amazing speed. | 그는 놀라운 속도로 달렸다. |
| [spel 스뻴] | How do you spell this word? | 이 단어의 철자가 어떻게 되나요? |
| [spend 스뻰드] | How much money do you spend? | 돈을 얼마나 썼니? |

## spoon
숟가락, 스푼
[spuːn 스푸-ㄴ]

spoon   spoon   spoon

## sport
스포츠
[spɔːrt 스포-올트]

sport   sport   sport

## spring
봄
[spriŋ 스프링]

spring   spring

## square
사각형
[skwɛər 스퀘어]

square   square   square

## stair
계단
[stɛər 스페어]

stair   stair   stair   stair

---

| | | |
|---|---|---|
| [spuːn 스푸-ㄴ] | I ate my meal with a spoon. | 나는 숟가락으로 식사를 했다. |
| [spɔːrt 스포-올트] | Soccer is a popular sport in Korea. | 한국에서 축구는 인기가 좋다. |
| [spriŋ 스프링] | I like spring. | 난 봄이 좋아요. |
| [skwɛər 스퀘어] | Its shape is square. | 이것의 모양은 사각형이다. |
| [stɛər 스페어] | I went up stairs. | 나는 계단을 올랐다. |

## stamp
우표, 인지
[stæmp스탬프]

stamp    stamp

## stand
서다, 일어서다
[stænd스탠드]

stand    stand    stand

## star
별
[staːr스따-ㄹ]

star    star    star    star

## start
출발하다
[staːrt스딸-트]

start    start    start

## station
역, 정거장
[stéiʃən스때이션]

station    station    station

---

| | | |
|---|---|---|
| [stæmp스탬프] | I like collecting stamps. | 나는 우표 수집을 좋아해요, |
| [stænd스탠드] | Stand up, please. | 일어서 주세요, |
| [staːr스따-ㄹ] | It is hard to see stars in the city. | 도시에서는 별을 보기 힘들다, |
| [staːrt스딸-트] | Let's start. | 시작하자, |
| [stéiʃən스때이션] | I wait for taxi at the station. | 나는 정거장에서 택시를 기다린다, |

## step
걸음
[step 스땝]

step　　step　　step　　step

## stop
멈추다
[stap 스땁]

stop　　stop　　stop　　stop

## store
가게, 상점
[stɔːr 스또어-ㄹ]

store　　store　　store　　store

## story
이야기
[stɔ́ːri 스토뤼]

story　　story　　story　　story

## strawberry
딸기
[strɔ́ːbéri 스뜨뤄-베뤼]

strawberry　　strawberry

| | | |
|---|---|---|
| [step 스땝] | I made a step forward. | 나는 한 걸음 앞으로 나아갔다. |
| [stap 스땁] | He stopped to talk. | 그는 이야기하기 위해 멈췄다. |
| [stɔːr 스또어-ㄹ] | I came in a fruit store. | 나는 과일 가게에 들렀다. |
| [stɔ́ːri 스토뤼] | Mom likes to tell me some stories. | 엄마는 나에게 얘기해 주시는 걸 좋아하신다. |
| [strɔ́ːbéri 스뜨뤄-베뤼] | I like strawberry. | 나는 딸기를 좋아해요. |

## street
거리
[striːt 스뜨뤼-ㅅ]

street    street    street

## strike
때리다
[straik 스뜨롸익]

strike    strike    strike

## strong
힘이 센, 강한
[strɔːŋ 스뜨뤄-엉]

strong    strong    strong

## student
학생
[stjúːdənt 스츄-던트]

student    student    student

## study
공부하다
[stʌ́di 스떠디]

study   study   study

| | | |
|---|---|---|
| [striːt 스뜨뤼-ㅅ] | Don't play in the street. | 도로에서 놀면 안 돼요. |
| [straik 스뜨롸익] | I strike a ball. | 나는 공을 친다. |
| [strɔːŋ 스뜨뤄-엉] | The boy looks strong. | 그 소년은 강해 보인다. |
| [stjúːdənt 스츄-던트] | How many student are there? | 학생이 몇 명 있죠? |
| [stʌ́di 스떠디] | At school, I study English. | 학교에서, 나는 영어를 공부한다. |

| | |
|---|---|
| **stupid**<br>어리석은<br>[stjú:pid스뚜피-드] | stupid     stupid     stupid |
| **subway**<br>지하철<br>[sʌ́bwéi써브웨이] | subway     subway     subway |
| **sugar**<br>설탕<br>[ʃúgər 슈걸] | sugar     sugar     sugar |
| **summer**<br>여름<br>[sʌ́mər써머ㄹ] | summer     summer  |
| **sun**<br>태양, 햇빛<br>[sʌn 썬] | sun     sun     sun     sun |

| | | |
|---|---|---|
| [stjú:pid스뚜피-드] | He is stupid. | 그는 어리석다. |
| [sʌ́bwéi써브웨이] | We went to In-cheon by subway. | 우리는 지하철로 인천에 갔다. |
| [ʃúgər 슈걸] | Do you like sugar in your coffee? | 커피에 설탕 넣으시겠어요? |
| [sʌ́mər써머ㄹ] | In summer, it is hot. | 여름에는 더워요. |
| [sʌn 썬] | The sun rises in the east. | 해는 동쪽에서 뜬다. |

147

**supermarket**
슈퍼마켓

[súːpərmáːrkit
수-퍼ㄹ말킷]

supermarket

**supper**
저녁식사

[sΛpər 써퍼얼]

supper    supper    supper

**sweater**
스웨터

[swétər 스웨터]

sweater    sweater    sweater

---

| [súːpərmáːrkit 수-퍼ㄹ말킷] | I went to a supermarket to buy corn. | 나는 옥수수를 사기위해 슈퍼마켓에 갔다. |
| [sΛpər 써퍼얼] | Supper is the last meal of the day. | 저녁식사는 하루의 마지막 식사이다. |
| [swétər 스웨터] | This sweater is warm. | 이 스웨터는 따뜻하다. |

**swim**
수영하다

[swim 스윔]

swim  swim  swim

**swing**
그네

[swiŋ 스윙]

swing  swing

**switch**
전기 스위치

[switʃ 스윗치]

switch  switch  switch

| | | |
|---|---|---|
| [swim 스윔] | We went swimming last Sunday. | 지난 일요일 우리는 수영하러 갔다. |
| [swiŋ 스윙] | There are two boys on the swing. | 그네에 남자아이 둘이 타고 있다. |
| [switʃ 스윗치]] | Switch off the light, please. | 불을 꺼 주세요. |

## table
테이블

[téibl 테이블]

table  table  table

## take
받다

[teik 테익]

take        take        take

## talk
말하다

[tɔːk 터-억]

talk      talk      talk      talk

## tall
키가 큰

[tɔːl 토-ㄹ]

tall      tall      tall      tall

| | | |
|---|---|---|
| [téibl 테이블] | There are two books on the table. | 테이블 위에 책이 2권 있다. |
| [teik 테익] | Take this letter to your mother. | 이 편지를 어머니께 가져다 드리렴. |
| [tɔːk 터-억] | She talks good English. | 그녀는 훌륭한 영어를 말한다. |
| [tɔːl 토-ㄹ] | He is tall. | 그는 키가 크다. |

**taste**
맛을 보다
[teist 테이스트]

taste　　taste　　taste

**taxi**
택시
[tǽksi 택씨]

taxi　　taxi　　taxi

**teach**
가르치다
[tiːtʃ 티-취]

teach　　teach　　teach

**team**
팀
[tiːm 팀]

team　　team　　team

**telephone**
전화
[téləfóun 텔레포운]

telephone　　telephone

| | | |
|---|---|---|
| [teist 테이스트] | It tastes sweet. | 단맛이 난다. |
| [tǽksi 택씨] | I took a taxi to the airport. | 공항까지 택시를 타고 갔다. |
| [tiːtʃ 티-취] | She teaches English at our school. | 그녀는 학교에서 영어를 가르친다. |
| [tiːm 팀] | His team won the game. | 그의 팀이 게임에서 이겼다. |
| [téləfóun 텔레포운] | He is on the telephone. | 그는 통화중이다. |

**television**
텔레비전
[téləvíʒən 텔리뷔젼]

television   television

**tell**
말하다
[tel 텔]

tell   tell   tell   tell

**tennis**
테니스
[ténis 테니스]

tennis   tennis   tennis

**test**
시험, 검사
[test 테스트]

test   test   test   test

**than**
~보다
[ðæn 덴]

than   than   than   than

| | | |
|---|---|---|
| [télvíʒən 텔리뷔젼] | I watched television. | 나는 텔레비전을 보았어요, |
| [tel 텔] | Don't tell a lie. | 거짓말을 하지 마라, |
| [ténis 테니스] | She played tennis with her friend. | 그녀는 친구와 함께 테니스를 쳤다, |
| [test 테스트] | I had a test last Friday. | 지난 금요일에 나는 시험을 봤다, |
| [ðæn 덴] | The box is bigger than me. | 그 상자는 나보다 크다, |

152

| | |
|---|---|
| **thank**<br>감사하다<br>[θæŋk 쌩크] | thank     thank     thank |
| **that**<br>저것, 그것<br>[ðæt 댓] | that     that     that |
| **the**<br>그<br>[ðə/ði 더] | the   the   the   the |
| **their**<br>그들의<br>[ðɛər 데얼] | their     their     their |
| **them**<br>그들을<br>[ðem 뎀] | them     them     them |

| | | |
|---|---|---|
| [θæŋk 쌩크] | Thank you very much. | 정말 감사합니다. |
| [ðæt 댓] | Look at that! That is big! | 저것좀 봐! 크다! |
| [ðə/ði 더] | The girl is my sister. | 그 소녀는 내 여동생입니다. |
| [ðɛər 데얼] | Their captain is very good. | 그들의 주장은 굉장히 좋은 사람이야. |
| [ðem 뎀] | I told them to wait. | 나는 그들에게 기다리라고 말했어요. |

**then**
그 때, 그러면
[ðen 덴]

then    then    then

**there**
거기에
[ðɛər 데얼]

there    there    there

**these**
이것들
[ðíːz 디−즈]

these    these    these

**they**
그들은
[ðei 데이]

they    they    they

**thick**
두꺼운
[θik 씩]

thick  thick  thick

| | | |
|---|---|---|
| [ðen 덴] | Father was a little child then. | 그 당시 아버지는 작은 어린아이였다. |
| [ðɛər 데얼] | Look over there. | 저기 좀 봐. |
| [ðíːz 디−즈] | These apples are red. | 이 사과들은 빨갛다. |
| [ðei 데이] | They are going to school. | 그들은 학교에 가고 있어요. |
| [θik 씩] | How thick is it? | 그건 두께가 얼마나 되죠? |

**thin**
얇은
[θin 띤]

thin    thin    thin

**thing**
것, 물건
[θiŋ 씽]

thing    thing    thing

**think**
~라고 생각하다
[θiŋk 씽크]

think    think    think

**this**
이것
[ðis 디쓰]

this    this    this

**those**
그것들
[ðouz 도즈]

those    those    those

---

| [θin 띤] | This book is very thin. | 이 책은 정말 얇아요. |
| [θiŋ 씽] | There are many things in the market. | 시장에는 많은 것들이 있다. |
| [θiŋk 씽크] | I think it is wrong. | 나는 그것이 틀렸다고 생각한다. |
| [ðis 디쓰] | How about this shirt? | 이 셔츠는 어때요? |
| [ðouz 도즈] | Those shoes are expensive. | 그 구두는 비싸다. |

## throw
던지다

[θrou 쓰로우]

throw　　　throw　　　throw

## ticket
표

[tíkit 티킷]

ticket　　　ticket　　　ticket

## tie
넥타이

[tai 타이]

tie　tie　tie　tie　tie

## tiger
호랑이

[táigər 타이걸]

tiger　　　tiger　　　tiger

## till
～까지

[til 틸]

till　　till　　till　　till　　till

| | | |
|---|---|---|
| [θrou 쓰로우] | The pitcher throw a ball to me. | 투수가 나에게 공을 던졌어요. |
| [tíkit 티킷] | Please show me your tickets. | 표 좀 보여주세요. |
| [tai 타이] | I must wear a tie tonight. | 저는 오늘 꼭 넥타이를 매야해요. |
| [táigər 타이걸] | Have you ever seen a tiger? | 너는 호랑이를 본적 있니? |
| [til 틸] | I will wait you till night. | 난 널 저녁까지 기다릴거야. |

## time
시각, 시간

[taim 타임]

time    time    time    time

## to
~에, ~로

[tu 투]

to   to   to   to   to   to

## today
오늘

[tudéi 투데이]

today    today    today

## tomato
토마토

[təméitou터메이토]

tomato    tomato

## tomorrow
내일

[təmɔ́ːrou투머-로우]

tomorrow    tomorrow

| | | |
|---|---|---|
| [taim 타임] | What time is it? | 지금 몇 시죠? |
| [tu 투] | I went to my grandmother's. | 나는 할머니 댁에 갔다. |
| [tudéi 투데이] | Today is my birthday. | 오늘은 내 생일이다. |
| [təméitou터메이토] | My mother likes tomato juice. | 엄마는 토마토주스를 좋아하세요. |
| [təmɔ́ːrou투머-로우] | Tomorrow will be cold. | 내일은 추울 거야. |

## tonight
오늘 밤

[tənáit 터나잇]

tonight　tonight　tonight

## too
~도 또한

[tu: 튜-]

too　too　too　too

## tooth
이, 치아

[tu:θ 투-쓰]

tooth　tooth　tooth

## top
정상

[tɔp 타프]

top　top　top　top　top

## travel
여행, 여행하다

[trǽvəl튜뢰블]

travel　travel

| | | |
|---|---|---|
| [tənáit 터나잇] | Tonight will be snowy. | 오늘밤엔 눈이 올 거야. |
| [tu: 튜-] | Me, too. | 나 또한 그래. |
| [tu:θ 투-쓰] | Brush tooth before you go to bed. | 자기전 이를 닦아라. |
| [tɔp 타프] | He reached the top of the mountain. | 그는 산꼭대기에 도착했다. |
| [trǽvəl튜뢰블] | I want to travel around the world. | 나는 전세계를 여행하고 싶어요. |

**town**
마을

[táun 타운]

town　town　town

**toy**
장난감

[tɔi 터이]

toy　toy　toy　toy

**train**
기차

[trein 츄뢰인]

train　train　train

**tree**
나무

[tri: 츄뤼-]

tree　tree　tree　tree

---

| | | |
|---|---|---|
| [táun 타운] | I lives in town. | 나는 마을에 살아요. |
| [tɔi 터이] | I played with toy. | 나는 장난감을 가지고 놀았다. |
| [trein 츄뢰인] | I will travel by train. | 나는 기차로 여행할거예요. |
| [tri: 츄뤼-] | The tree is older than me. | 저 나무는 나보다 나이가 많아요. |

**trip**
여행
[trip 츄뤼ㅂ]

trip     trip     trip     trip

**truck**
트럭
[trʌk 츄럭]

truck     truck     truck

**try**
시도, 시도하다
[trɑi 츄롸이]

try     try     try     try

**tulip**
튤립
[tjúːlip 튜울립]

tulip     tulip     tulip     tulip

| | | |
|---|---|---|
| [trip 츄뤼ㅂ] | How was your trip? | 여행 어땠니? |
| [trʌk 츄럭] | The truck is big. | 저 트럭은 크다. |
| [trɑi츄롸이] | Let's try this. | 이거 해보자(이거 시도해보자) |
| [tjúːlip 튜울립] | I like tulips. | 나는 튤립을 좋아한다. |

## Uu

| | |
|---|---|
| **umbrella**<br>우산<br>[ʌmbrélə엄브륄러] | umbrella  umbrella  |
| **uncle**<br>아저씨, 삼촌<br>[ʌ́ŋkl 엉끌] | uncle       uncle       uncle |
| **under**<br>~의 아래에<br>[ʌ́ndər 언덜] | under       under       under |

| | | |
|---|---|---|
| [ʌmbrélə엄브륄러] | He has an umbrella in his hand. | 그의 손에 우산이 있다(그는 우산을 들고 있어요), |
| [ʌ́ŋkl 엉끌] | I am going to my uncle's. | 나는 삼촌댁에 갈 거예요, |
| [ʌ́ndər 언덜] | There are ants under the tree. | 나무 아래 개미들이 있어요, |

## up
위쪽으로

[ʌp 엎]

up   up   up   up   up

## us
우리들을

[ʌs 어쓰]

us   us   us   us   us

[ʌp 엎]

Stand up please.

일어서 주세요.

[ʌs 어쓰]

He told us to stay home.

그는 우리에게 집에 있으라고 했다.

162

## very
매우, 아주

[véri 붸뤼]

very    very    very    very

## video
비디오

[vídioú브이디오]

video    video    video

## village
마을, 촌락

[vílidʒ 빌리쥐]

village    village    village

---

| [véri 붸뤼] | I like it very much. | 난 그것을 매우 좋아해요. |
| [vídioú브이디오] | How often do you rent video tapes? | 당신은 얼마나 자주 비디오 테이프를 빌려요? |
| [vílidʒ 빌리쥐] | The farmer lives in the village. | 그 농부는 마을에 살아요. |

**violin**
바이올린

[váiəlín봐이얼린]

violin   violin   violin

**visit**
방문하다

[vízit 뷔짓]

visit   visit   very   visit

| | | |
|---|---|---|
| [váiəlín봐이얼린] | I can play the violin. | 저는 바이올린을 연주할 수 있어요. |
| [vízit 뷔짓] | Can you visit me, today? | 오늘 절 방문해 줄 수 있나요? |

**W w**

| | |
|---|---|
| **wait**<br>기다리다<br>[weit 웨잇] | wait    wait    wait  |
| **walk**<br>걷다, 산책하다<br>[wɔːk 워–억] | walk    walk    walk    walk |
| **wall**<br>벽<br>[wɔːl 워–얼] | wall    wall    wall    wall |
| **want**<br>원하다, 바라다<br>[wɔːnt 원트] | want    want    want    want |

| | | |
|---|---|---|
| [weit 웨잇] | Min-ho waits for his girl friend. | 민호는 그의 여자 친구를 기다립니다, |
| [wɔːk 워–억] | I walk in the park with my wife. | 나는 아내와 공원을 걷는다, |
| [wɔːl 워–얼] | The mirror hangs on the wall. | 그 거울은 벽에 걸려있다, |
| [wɔːnt 원트] | I want to some water. | 나는 물을 마시고 싶다, |

165

## warm
따뜻한

[wɔːrm 워-ㄹ엄]

warm　　warm　　warm

## was
am, is의과거형

[wʌz 워즈]

was　　was　　was　　was

## watch
손목시계

[watʃ 왓취]

watch　　　watch

## water
물

[wɔ́ːtər 워-터]

water　　water　　water

## way
길, 방법

[wei 웨이]

way　　way　　way　　way

---

| | | |
|---|---|---|
| [wɔːrm 워-ㄹ엄] | Today is warm. | 오늘은 따뜻하다. |
| [wʌz 워즈] | He was a student. | 그는 학생이었다. |
| [watʃ 왓취] | My watch is old. | 내 시계는 낡았다. |
| [wɔ́ːtər 워-터] | People drink water every day. | 사람들은 물을 매일 마신다. |
| [wei 웨이] | There is no way through. | 통로가 없어요. |

## we
우리, 저희가
[w i: 위-]

we we we we

## weak
약한
[w í:k 위-크]

weak weak weak

## week
주, 1주간
[w i:k 위-크]

week week week

## welcome
환영하다
[wélkəm 웰컴]

welcome welcome

## well
만족하게, 잘
[w el 웰]

well well well well

---

| | | |
|---|---|---|
| [w i: 위-] | We go to school at 8 o'clock. | 우리는 8시에 등교한다. |
| [w í:k 위-크]? | Tom is weak. | Tom은 (체력이)약해요. |
| [w i:k 위-크]? | I will travel America for a week. | 나는 일주일 동안 미국을 여행할 거야. |
| [wélkəm 웰컴] | Welcome to Korea! | 한국에 오신 걸 환영합니다! |
| [w el 웰] | He speaks English very well. | 그는 영어를 아주 잘한다. |

**were**
are의 과거형
[wɜːr 워-ㄹ]

were　　　were　　　were

**west**
서쪽
[west 웨스트]

west　west　west

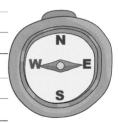

**wet**
젖은, 축축한
[wet 웨ㅌ]

wet　　wet　　　wet　　　wet

**what**
무엇, 어떤
[hwat 왓]

what　　　what　　　what

**when**
언제
[hwen 웬]

when　　　when　　　when

| | | |
|---|---|---|
| [wɜːr 워-ㄹ] | We were students. | 우리는 학생이었다. |
| [west 웨스트] | The sun sets in the west. | 해는 서쪽으로 진다. |
| [wet 웨ㅌ] | We have the wet season in June. | 6월은 장마철이다. |
| [hwat 왓] | What are you doing? | 뭐하고 있니? |
| [hwen 웬] | When is your birthday? | 생일이 언제야? |

## where
어디에

[hwεər 웨얼]

where     where     where

## which
어느쪽, 어느

[hwitʃ 윗취]

which     which     which

## white
흰, 흰빛

[hwait 와이트]

white     white     white

## who
누구

[hu: 후-]

who    who    who

## whom
누구를

[huːm 후우-ㅁ]

whom     whom     whom

| [hwεər 웨얼] | Where are you from? | 어디 출신이야? |
| [hwitʃ 윗취] | Which one is better? | 어떤게 더 좋아? |
| [hwait 와이트] | We can see the white color in the dark. | 우리는 어둠 속에서 흰색을 볼 수 있다. |
| [hu: 후-] | Who is he? | 그는 누구야? |
| [huːm 후우-ㅁ] | Whom did you meet yesterday? | 어제 누구를 만났어? |

## whose
누구의

[huːz 후-즈]

whose   whose   whose

## why
왜

[hwai 와이]

why   why   why   why

## wide
넓은

[waid 와이드]

wide   wide   wide

## win
이기다

[win 윈]

win   win   win   win

| | | |
|---|---|---|
| [huːz 후-즈] | Whose daughter is she? | 누구의 딸이야? |
| [hwai 와이] | Why do you cry? | 왜 우니? |
| [waid 와이드] | That place is wide. | 그곳은 넓어요. |
| [win 윈] | You win! | 네가 이겼어! |

**wind**
바람
[wind 윈드]

wind  wind  wind

**window**
창(창문)
[wíndou 윈도우]

window  window

**wing**
날개
[wiŋ 윙]

wing  wing  wing

**winter**
겨울
[wíntər 윈터얼]

winter  winter  winter

| | | |
|---|---|---|
| [wind 윈드] | The paper is swing in the wind. | 그 종이가 바람에 흔들린다. |
| [wíndou 윈도우] | Please open the window. | 창문 좀 열어 주세요. |
| [wiŋ 윙] | Birds have wings. | 새들은 날개를 가지고 있다. |
| [wíntər 윈터얼] | It's cold in winter. | 겨울은 추워요. |

**wood**
나무, 숲
[wud 우드]

wood   wood   wood

**word**
낱말, 단어
[wəːrd 워드]

word   word   word

**world**
세계, 지구
[wəːrld 워-ㄹ드]

world  world   world

---

[wud 우드]　　　I walked in the wood.　　　나는 숲속을 걸었어요.

[wəːrd 워드]　　How do you spell this word?　　이 단어 철자가 어떻게 되죠?

[wəːrld 워-ㄹ드]　I want to travel all over the world.　나는 전 세계를 여행하고 싶다.

**year**
년, 나이
[jiər 이얼]

year　　　year　　　year

**yellow**
노랑
[jélou 옐로-]

yellow　　　yellow

**yes**
예, 네
[jes 예스]

yes　yes　yes　yes　yes

**yesterday**
어제
[jéstərdéi예스털데이]

yesterday　　　yesterday

| [jiər 이얼] | Happy new year! | 새해 복 많이 받으세요! |
| [jélou 옐로-] | The color of bananas is yellow. | 바나나는 노랑색이다. |
| [jes 예스] | Yes, ma'am. | 네, 선생님 |
| [jéstərdéi예스털데이] | Yesterday was my brother's birthday. | 어제는 내 남동생의 생일이었다. |

## you
너, 당신

[ juː 유-]

you  you  you  you

## young
젊은, 어린

[ jʌŋ 영]

young  young  young

## your
너의, 너희들의

[ juər 유얼]

your  your  your

## yours
너의 것

[ juərz 유어즈]

yours  yours  yours

## yourself
너 자신의

[ juərsélf유어쎌프]

yourself  yourself

| | | |
|---|---|---|
| [ juː 유-] | You look so pretty. | 너는 굉장히 예쁘다(너는 참 예쁘구나). |
| [ jʌŋ 영] | He is young. | 그는 어리다. |
| [ juər 유얼] | What is your name? | 너의 이름은 무엇이니? |
| [ juərz 유어즈] | Yours is beautiful. | 너의 것은 예쁘다. |
| [ juərsélf유어쎌프] | You should know yourself. | 너는 네 자신을 알아야 한다. |

Z z

| zero | zero   zero   zero   zero |
|------|---------------------------|
| 0, 영 | |
| [zíərou 지어로우] | |

| ZOO | ZOO   ZOO   ZOO   ZOO |
|------|---------------------------|
| 동물원 | |
| [zu: 주-] | |

| [zíərou 지어로우] | '0' is called zero. | 0은 영이라고 부른다, |
|---|---|---|
| [zu: 주-] | Let's go to the zoo. | 동물원에 가자, |

교과부 지정

새로 만든
**영단어 800**

**초판 발행** 2018년 11월 10일

**글** 편집부

**펴낸이** 서영희 | **펴낸곳** 와이 앤 엠

**편집** 임명아

**본문인쇄** 신화 인쇄 | **제책** 세림 제책

**제작** 이윤식 | **마케팅** 강성태

**주소** 120-100 서울시 서대문구 홍은동 376-28

**전화** (02)308-3891 | Fax (02)308-3892

**E-mail** yam3891@naver.com

**등록** 2007년 8월 29일 제312-2007-00004호

ISBN 978-89-93557-90-9  63710